LIGHTS
TO THE
WORLD

By the same author:

C. H. Spurgeon: Pastor/Evangelist
(Baptist Historical Society, 1992)

LIGHTS TO THE WORLD

A History of
Spurgeon's College
1856—1992

Mike Nicholls

BD, MTh, MPhil, Baptist Pastor

Published in Association with

NUPRINT
HARPENDEN, HERTS

© Rev. M.K. Nicholls 1993

First published in 1994.

All rights reserved.

Apart from any fair dealing for the purposes of research or
private study, or criticism or review, as permitted under the
Copyright, Designs and Patents Act, 1988, this publication
may be reproduced, stored or transmitted, in any forms or by
any means, only with the prior permission in writing of the
publishers, or in the case of reprographic reproduction
in accordance with the terms of licences issued by the Copyright
Licensing Agency. Enquiries concerning reproduction outside
those terms should be sent to the publishers at the
undermentioned address.

ISBN 0 9522641 0 2

British Library Cataloguing-in-Publication Data
A catalogue record for this book
is available from the British Library

Designed and produced in England for Rev. M.K. Nicholls by
Nuprint Ltd, Station Road, Harpenden, Herts AL5 4SE

*This book is dedicated to my wife Diana and
our children Emma, Helen and Tim
whose unfailing encouragement in my ministry
has been of tremendous value.*

Contents

List of Illustrations	9
List of Abbreviations and Tables	10
List of College Staff	11
Foreword by Clive Calver	15
Acknowledgements	17
Introduction	19
1. The Governor	27
2. The Institution: 1856—1892	51
3. The Tabernacle: 1892—1922	98
4. The Brethren: 1923—1957	134
5. The Ministry: 1958—1992	168
Notes	197
Bibliography	207

Illustrations

Fig. 1.1   C.H. Spurgeon in 1854 after he became the minister of New Park Street Chapel, Southwark.
Fig. 1.2   The facade of the Metropolitan Tabernacle built in 1859 to house the congregations attracted to Spurgeon.
Fig. 1.3   The old Pastors' College built in 1874 and vacated in 1923.
Fig. 1.4   Rev. Charles Haddon Spurgeon, the founder and first President of the College 1856–1892.
Fig. 1.5   A score from C.H. Spurgeon's Friday afternoon pastoral lectures to the students.
Fig. 2.1   The Rev. James Archer Spurgeon, DD LLD, the second President of the College 1892–1896.
Fig. 2.2   Former Presidents and Tutors of the old Pastors' College.
Fig. 2.3   C.H. Spurgeon with former students in 1888, including the first college student, Tom Medhurst, on the extreme right in the front row.
Fig. 2.4   A typical group of late nineteenth-century students.
Fig. 3.1   The Rev. Thomas Spurgeon, the third President of the College 1896–1917.
Fig. 3.2   Council, staff and students, 1922.
Fig. 3.3   Professor W.H. Gaussen, MA, LLB (1898–1938); Principal A. McCaig, BA, LLD (1898–1925); Professor P.W. Evans, BA, BD (1922–1925).
Fig. 3.4   South view—Spurgeon's College (1922).
Fig. 4.1   Application: concerning admission to the college.
Fig. 4.2   First resident students, the tutors and wardens (1923).
Fig. 4.3   Chapel stone-laying.
Fig. 4.4   The College chapel.
Fig. 4.5   A quiet place.
Fig. 4.6   Entrance Hall—when occupied by the donor, C. Hay Walker.
Fig. 4.7   Principal Percival Evans, BA, DD (1925–1950).
Fig. 4.8   Principal Frederick Cawley, BA, BD, PhD (1950–1955).
Fig. 5.1   Principal Eric H. Worstead, MA, BD, MTh, PhD (1956–1958).
Fig. 5.2   Principal George R. Beasley-Murray, MA, PhD, DD (1958–1973).
Fig. 5.3   Principal, staff and students (1965).
Fig. 5.4   Principal Raymond Brown, MA, BD, MTh, PhD (1973–1986).
Fig. 5.5   Principal Paul Beasley-Murray, MA, PhD (1988–1992).
Fig. 5.6   Spurgeon's College (1992).

Abbreviations

ACA	Associate of the Institute of Chartered Accountants
BA	Bachelor of Arts
BSc	Bachelor of Science
DD	Doctor of Divinity
Dip Th	Diploma in Theology
DSO	Distinguished Service Order
DTL	Doctor of Theology
FCA	Fellow of the Institute of Chartered Accountants
MC	Member of Congress, Master of Ceremonies, Member of Council, Military Cross
LLB	Bachelor of Laws
LLD	Doctor of Laws
MD	Doctor of Medicine
MTL	Master of Theology
M Phil	Master of Philosophy
OBE	Officer of the Order of the British Empire
PhD	Doctor of Philosophy
STP–STh	Professor of Theology

Tables

Table 1.1 Time Table, 1927
Table 2.1 Curriculum for 1930—31
Table 3.1 College Structure

College Staff List

PRESIDENTS

Charles Haddon Spurgeon	1856–1892
James Archer Spurgeon, DD, LLD	1892–1896
Thomas Spurgeon	1896–1917

PRINCIPALS

George Rogers	1856–1881
David Gracey	1881–1893
Archibald McCaig, BA, LLD	1898–1925
Percy William Evans, BA, DD	1925–1950
Frederick Cawley, BA, BD, PhD	1950–1955
Eric H. Worstead, BA, BD, MTh	1955–1957
George R. Beasley-Murray, MA, PhD, DD	1958–1973
Raymond Brown, MA, BD, MTh, PhD	1973–1986
Paul Beasley-Murray, MA, PhD	1986–1992

TUTORS

David Gracey	1862–1881
Archibald Fergusson	1862–1892
Frederick George Marchant	1881–1898
John E. Ewing, MA, DD	1891–1893
Archibald McCaig, BA, LLD	1892–1898
William Usher, MD	1893–1898
Walter Hackney, MA	1898–1925
William Hardy Gaussen, MA, LLB	1898–1938
Percy William Evans, BA, BD	1922–1925
James Frederick Taviner, BA	1925–1938
D. Russell Smith	1928–1932
Frederick Cawley, BA, BD, PhD	1938–1950
Ronald Arthur Ward, MA, BD, PhD	1938–1949
Eric Henry Worstead, BA, BD, MTh	1946–1955
William Graham Scroggie, DD	1948–1952
George R. Beasley-Murray, BA, BD, MTh, PhD	1950–1956
Geoffrey W. Rusling, MA, BD	1951–1971
Stanley J. Dewhurst, BD, MTh	1955–1979
Frank S. Fitzsimmonds, BA, BD, MTh	1956–1983
Rex A. Mason, MA, BD, PhD	1965–1975

Lewis A. Drummond, BA, BD, MTh, PhD	1968–1973
Raymond Brown, MA, BD, MTh, PhD	1971–1973
Bruce A. Milne, MA, BD, PhD	1974–1983
Peter D. Manson, BSc, BD	1975–1991
Martin J. Selman, BA, MA, PhD	1975–
Michael K. Nicholls, BD, MTh, M Phil	1976–1991
John F. Maile, BD	1974–1988
Brian Stanley, MA, PhD	1979–1991
Robert J. Thompson, BA, BD, ThM, D Theol, MA	1984–1987
Debra K. Reid, BD, MA, PhD	1987–
Nigel Wright, BA, BD, MTh	1987–
Stuart B. Christine, MA, BA	1988–1991
R. Alastair Campbell, MA	1989–
Colin A. Brown, BD, MA, PhD, STh	1990–
Robert W.F. Archer, BA, BD	1990–
Arthur Rowe, MA, MTh	1991–
William Allen, BA	1991–
Stuart Murray, LLB, Dip Th	1992–
Ian Randall, MA, M Phil	1992–

CHAIRMEN OF COUNCIL

John Bradford	1919—1926
Thomas Greenwood	1926—1935
F.J.H. Humphrey, DSO	1935—1947
F.J. Walkey, OBE, MC	1947—1949
W. Harold Tebbit	1950—1957
W. Charles Johnson	1957—1970
C.R. Goulding	1970—1976
John J. Brown, BD	1976—1978
George Cumming, BD	1978—1986
Arthur Thompson, BD	1986—1987
David Harper, BD	1987—

TREASURERS

W.C. Murrell and J. Passmore	1876—1882
Thomas H. Olney	1882—1900
Frank Thompson	1900—1936
Albert W. Mills, FCA,	1937—1953
W.R. Booth, ACA, ASAA	1953—1982
David R. Lewis	1982—1988
Bryan K. Rogers	1988—

SECRETARIES

C. Blackshaw	1876—1879
C.H Thomas	1880—1885
H. Hibbert	1885—1892
E.H. Bartlett	1893—1915
John H Weeks	1916—1925
Fred H. King	1925—1926
Ernest E. Welton	1927—1937
G.W. Harte	1937—1954
Geoffrey W. Rusling, MA, BD	1954—1962
Ernest Willmott	1962—1972
Wilfred Roper	1972—1978
John J. Brown, BD	1978—1982
David Harrison	1982—

FOREWORD

IT MAY SEEM STRANGE for a graduate of London Bible College to be writing the foreword to a history of Spurgeon's College!

This becomes less surprising when one considers the story of what was originally called the Pastors' College, especially when it is placed in its historical context. For Spurgeon's has not just contributed to the life of the Baptist denomination—the impact of the college has been felt throughout the evangelical community world-wide as contemporary issues such as church planting, ministerial training and theological scholarship have been at the heart of the story.

In the ensuing pages the reader will meet Charles Haddon Spurgeon in the context of the society to which he ministered. Furthermore Spurgeon's dream of equipping fresh generations of reformed pastors is explored, and its value is succinctly evaluated. It is never enough to be concerned with one's own times; each of us has a responsibility for the future. This was a fact that Spurgeon acknowledged, and the College today is a part of his legacy to the twentieth century and beyond.

Some find history to be boring. But the lessons to be learned from it are invaluable. Mike Nicholls has made an important contribution to our thinking about training future leaders. He has not written a eulogy of the College. Instead he explains its successes and failures in order that we might all learn for the future.

If current evangelical developments in the United Kingdom are to progress on a firm foundation then we need a new generation of able, trained and qualified spiritual leaders. In this significant endeavour Spurgeon's will continue to play a vital role. Beyond its own training courses it has served as an example to others. Perhaps the lessons of the story of this college will enable others to avoid its mistakes and emulate its achievements.

This story shows that God does surprising things among his people. He chooses to fulfil his purposes through lives dedicated to his service. At the close of one phase he raises up fresh men and women to build on the past and write a new chapter. For Spurgeon's such a moment lies ahead in these closing years of the twentieth century.

These pages resonate with the joy of training leaders. Those leaders of tomorrow will owe a debt of gratitude to the legacy they receive from previous generations. All can rejoice in what God has done, can appreciate relevant lessons from history, and get ready for what God has in store for his Church in the twenty-first century.

But not if we forget our past!

Clive Calver
London, 1992

ACKNOWLEDGEMENTS

IN COMPLETING THIS WORK I'm very grateful for the encouragement of former colleagues and students at Spurgeon's College where I was pleased to serve for fifteen years.

I am especially grateful for the help and insight of many former students of the college who were glad to give me their recollections of the past.

Rev. J.J. Brown who knows more about Spurgeon and has done more for the college than any other person has carefully scrutinised the work to enhance its quality. Mrs Faith Bowers, whose editorial skills have avoided many mistakes, has used her objectivity to give balance to the work.

I am also grateful to the staff of the library at Spurgeon's College where much of the resource material, used to research the book, resides.

If any readers want to follow up particular matters, that are dealt with in the book, the college librarian would be the person to contact.

Countless other people have assisted in the production of this book and I want them to know how grateful I am. Geoffrey Rusling has done extensive research into early Baptist education and his help with the introductory material is gratefully acknowledged.

INTRODUCTION

DOUBT AND SELF-DOUBT play a more important part in the story of the Victorian ministry than the confident stories of many nineteenth-century churches would suggest. Ministry became more professional as clergy concentrated on specialist religious functions. But in the eyes of society the clergy were regarded less highly as a profession in 1900 than in 1800. Law and medicine offered more attractive opportunities socially and academically. Further, the challenges to Christian orthodoxy provoking intellectual doubt, brood over the story of the ministerial student and practitioner like a series of clouds—some lighter than others, but all threatening.

The nineteenth century was both colourful and formative. The tempo of change was great and development was complex. Whereas the leaves of a tree may attract us, the roots are the ultimately inescapable source. Therefore, in this book an attempt is made not simply to describe the formation of ministerial character and function through collegiate training but to analyse its various roots and note the interaction of social, educational, theological, denominational and personal factors that bore fruit in ministerial achievement. Commenting on pastoral training in London in 1856, C.H. Spurgeon said:

> No college at that time appeared to me to be suitable for the class of men that Providence and the Grace of God drew around me. They were mostly poor and most of the colleges involved neces-

sarily a considerable outlay to the student; for even where the education was free, books, clothes and other incidental expenses required a considerable sum per annum. Moreover, it must be frankly admitted that my views of the gospel and of the mode of training preachers were, and are, somewhat peculiar. I may have been uncharitable in my judgement but I thought the Calvinism of the theology usually taught to be very doubtful and the spiritual fervour of the students to be far behind their literary attainments.[1]

In this statement Spurgeon indicates the haphazard yet, as he would have said, divinely-ordained establishment of a new pattern of pastoral training in London.

Unlike Congregational ministerial training which was rooted in the institutional academies, the long and varied history of Baptist ministerial training displays a more fragmented and diverse approach.

Possibly the first Baptist academy for the purpose of ministerial training was superintended by John Davison at Trowbridge in the late seventeenth or early eighteenth century.[2] About 1732 a general preparatory school was established at Trosnant, Pontypool, Carmarthenshire, by John Griffiths, who was at the time manager of the Iron Works at Pontypool. The tuition of prospective ministerial students continued to be an important function of this institution for over forty years.[3] The school conducted by John Sutcliff, minister at Olney from 1775 to 1814, was primarily for ministerial students, of whom Sutcliff trained thirty-seven. Twelve of them went overseas as missionaries, among them William Carey, who as an 'out-pupil' received his first lessons in Latin from Sutcliff.[4]

The General Baptist Society for the Education of Young Men for the Ministry[5] started its work around 1792. The four tutors known to have worked for the Society trained about thirty-six men in all. The charismatic figure was Dan Taylor. No formal curriculum or examiners' report illuminates the training given by him in the early years of the Mile End Academy, but an address given in 1806 gives us clear indication of it. Taylor expressed the view that priority should be given to three studies: the English tongue, the Bible and the work of the Christian ministry. He believed that systematic theology, as it would be called today, was one of the vital subjects for instruction. The shortness of the course prevented the students from making any great progress in Greek and Hebrew, though we may venture to say that the progress which several of them made was considerable especially considering the other demands upon their time.

Concern for theological education was also expressed through financial provision. Francis Bampfield, who organised a Seventh-Day Baptist church at Bethnal Green, bequeathed his library in 1676 to promote a 'Design of Training up Young Men in Scripture Learning'.[6] Baptists also raised funds corporately, and individuals left monies to assist in ministerial training. In September 1689, after the passing of the Toleration Act, an assembly of Particular Baptists who met in London agreed to raise a fund, the purpose of which included the assistance of men who were 'disposed for study, having inviting gifts and are sound in fundamentals, in attaining to the knowledge and understanding of the languages of Latin, Greek and Hebrew.'[7] Two years later it was reported that 'several pious and hopeful men have been assisted in their acquirement of learning.'[8] It seems that shortly after this the interest of London Baptists in these broadly-based plans for a national assembly diminished.[9] The churches in the

West Country, however, continued to hold an annual assembly at Bristol or Taunton, and the Bristol Baptist Fund, founded in 1717, included the education of ministers among its purposes.[10] Meanwhile six London churches responded to an appeal which led in 1717 to the founding of the Particular Baptist Fund.[11]

Its training method, as funds permitted, was to place students under the tuition of selected ministers.[12]

Another centre was 'the London Baptist Education Society for Assisting Students' which was formed after a meeting held on 6 August 1752.[13] It had a somewhat chequered career until in 1805 the sole surviving trustee transferred its capital to the Particular Baptist Fund, with the proviso that it should be devoted to the Fund's educational work.[14]

Of educational trusts formed by individuals perhaps the best known is that founded by John Ward,[15] professor of rhetoric at Gresham College, in a Deed dated 11 July 1754. By it the founder sought to secure for appropriate candidates opportunities for 'improving in Latin, Greek and Hebrew and other studies suited to the Profession of Divinity'. Preference was to be given to Baptist applicants. Those accepted were to be sent to one of the Scottish universities, Ward himself expressing a preference for Edinburgh.[16]

Apart from the Bristol Academy founded in 1679, the opportunities for theological training within the Baptist denomination at the beginning of the nineteenth century were not abundant. However as the century progressed the number of Baptist institutions for ministerial training proliferated.

For Baptists it was important that a minister had spiritual qualifications, conversion and call. The early Baptists denied that the right to preach was tied to an office, hierarchical approval or adequate education. The first Baptist church, founded by John Smyth in 1608, had as its three recognised leaders a graduate, a lawyer and a furrier. William Kiffin, another leading Baptist, confidently preached, never having been to university nor having received episcopal orders.[17] These views do not indicate a suspicion of education so much as a conviction that human forms and ordinances could interfere with the operation of the Holy Spirit. Some early Baptists did receive university education and most preachers were encouraged to learn the biblical languages. In 1675 the Particular Baptists wanted to seek ways of 'providing an orderly standing ministry in the church who might give themselves to reading and study and so become able ministers of the New Testament'.[18] In the eighteenth century most agreed that 'human learning was useful'[19] but its essential character was questioned with the rise of scientific enquiry, the study of modern languages and theological speculation. With the Evangelical awakening, it became increasingly obvious that the hope of Christian expansion lay in a well-trained, dedicated ministry which would devote its God-given gifts to the evangelisation of the whole world. Vocation and education had to remain complementary. Andrew Fuller said he would support the Stepney Academy 'if he were able to presuppose the faith of Christ and the gifts suited to the ministry would accompany such work'.[20] He dreaded an unconverted ministry. Isaac Mann stressed the evangelistic purpose of education.[21] and the Bristol College course was designed to promote fruitful preaching.[22] To this end, William Jones was clear that scriptural knowledge must be the centre-piece of education.[23]

In 1885 an historical survey was written of the work of the Regent's Park Institution. Linked to the Baptist Fund, which was started in 1717 'to train able and well-qualified persons to defend the truth',[24] the college's effectiveness between 1855 and 1885 could be measured in terms of 'the numbers they have won for God'.[25] The eighteenth-century opinion that 'to be destitute of learning has been esteemed a good proof of a preacher's mission from above'[26] was no longer widely held. In 1825 at the Baptist church at Soham, Cambridgeshire, 'the people determined to obtain an educated man whose learning and talents they hoped might, under the blessing of God, tend to elevate the cause from its depressed state', and to this end consulted the 'Tutors of the Baptists College at Stepney'.[27]

The need for apologetic on the subject of educating ministers had not disappeared entirely. In 1831 a letter was addressed to the *Baptist Magazine*, reflecting the views of a church with a ministerial candidate where the pastor and deacons were averse to a course of academic instruction.[28] The answer gave cautious arguments in favour of such instruction. In 1848 Regent's Park College offered reassurance on the basis of the evangelistic[29] and spiritual aim of the institution and the judicious choice of candidates.[30] Within the Regent's tradition, vocation and education were well-balanced. Spiritual gifts and sanctified character were considered indispensable to the calling and effective ministry of a Baptist pastor whose fruitful preaching and peaceable relationships were crucial to harmony in the local church. The on-going story of the training of such pastors at Spurgeon's College is the subject of this book.

Fig. 1.1 C.H. Spurgeon in 1854 after he became the minister of New Park Street Chapel, Southwark.

CHAPTER 1

The Governor

THE EARLY HISTORY of the College was haphazard, 'a romance of faith'.[1] At his own church, the Metropolitan Tabernacle, C.H. Spurgeon saw a need 'to help preachers become better ones'.[2] The first student was a recently converted ropemaker, T.W. Medhurst. He began to come weekly to his pastor for several hours' instruction in theology. He was boarded with Rev. C.H. Hosken of Crayford and supported with money out of Spurgeon's own salary. Then he was put under the full-time tuition of Rev. George Rogers of Camberwell. At this point Spurgeon 'had not even a remote idea whereunto the college would grow',[3] but he began to arrange tuition for other young men.

Novel methods did not lead to isolationism. Indeed, Spurgeon said, 'In all other institutions doing similar work we take the deepest interest and shall continue to do so'.[4] He was a keen supporter of 'the college principle', frequently extolling its virtues from historical antecedents.[5] George Rogers wrote an article in 1884 on 'The scripturalness of the Pastors' College'.[6] He surveyed the evidence from Samuel to Paul and from Wycliffe to Wesley, concluding, 'The College...is in perfect accordance with the method by which the gospel was commanded to be preached to all nations. But he also made two important provisos. He highlighted the link of the Pastors' College with the pastorate of a local church, commenting that this is 'rarely exemplified'. Using the example of Doddridge's academy he also warned against colleges becoming too formal and legalistic: 'The Academy sought to make ministers rather than to aid them. It was not so successful, therefore, as it might otherwise have been.' Thus 'Colleges for the Christian ministry are Scriptural in proportion as they are prompted and controlled by that ministry.' But Nonconformity in the nineteenth century had often made its colleges centres of learning rather than religion. Therefore Spurgeon's College was distinctively different.

Educational Principles

'Encourage and help the colleges more and more,' Spurgeon advised, 'but see to it that those you aid are seminaries for the growth of unmistakeable gospel preachers.'[7] At the Metropolitan Tabernacle the Pastor found around him many young men 'earnest'[8] in tone with an irresistible urge to preach the gospel. Their only 'sad hindrance'[9] was a lack of education. Nothing would dampen their enthusiasm and Spurgeon wanted to improve their slender attainments and consequent effectiveness through education.

The primary objective of the Pastors' College was to make preachers of the gospel. No man was accepted for training unless he was naturally fitted to preaching, and, as far as could be judged, divinely called to that office. No amount of mental ability or scholastic achievement could make up for the absence of this. 'Our institution,' Spurgeon said, 'aims to keep out of the sacred office those who are not called to it. We are continually declining candidates because we question

Fig. 1.2 The facade of the Metropolitan Tabernacle built in 1859 to house the congregations attracted to Spurgeon.

their fitness. Some of these have education and money and are supported by earnest requests from parents and friends, but all this avails them nothing!'[10] He would not tolerate 'a low state of piety, a want of enthusiasm, a failure in private devotion, a lack of concentration'.[11]

It became a principle that before going to college 'a man must, during about two years, have been engaged in preaching and must have some seals to his ministry before we could entertain his application.'[12] This was because 'we wanted not men whom tutors could make into scholars but men whom the Lord had ordained to be preachers.'[13] Literary achievement was not undervalued but neither was it considered indispensable; it was always to be employed to a higher end: 'The present age...demands earnest and faithful preachers of the gospel irrespective of literary titles and qualifications.'[14] The all-controlling aim of the instruction given was the preparation of powerful preachers. Academic prestige alone was discarded; loss of intellectual respectability was risked; the curriculum was divorced from university degrees. 'There is a learning that is essential to be a successful ministry, namely the learning of the whole Bible to know God, by prayer, and experience of His dealings.'[15]

Spurgeon declared emphatically, 'Our men seek to preach efficiently, to get to the heart of the masses, to evangelise the poor—this is the College ambition, this and nothing else.'[16] The world might educate men for its own purposes but the Church must instruct men for its special service. 'We aim at helping men to set forth the truth of God.'[17] But if all students had to be preachers, Spurgeon ensured that all preachers could be students. He was training 'men of the people'.[18] As long as they had 'genuine talent'[19] he did not 'greatly concern himself in regard to...educational shortcomings'. He admitted there was a 'lowering of the average of scholarship' but believed that 'the shrewd common-sense, rough and ready brother is usually the successful man.'[20]

The educational principle of training only those who were preachers required defence from twin attacks. These came from people who, in Spurgeon's opinion, undervalued or overvalued education.

> Time was when an educated ministry was looked upon by certain of our brethren as a questionable blessing; indeed it was thought

Fig. 1.3 The Old Pastors' College built in 1874 and vacated in 1923.

that the less a minister knew the better, for there was then the more room for him to be taught by God. From the fact that God does not need man's wisdom it was inferred that He does need man's ignorance.... This depreciation of learning was a natural recoil from the folly which magnified education into a kind of deity.[21]

It was acknowledged that God used the preaching of unlearned men, but as a rule among their own class. In an age of general education, men would be selected who would not drive away their hearers by glaring ignorance of the simplest rules of correct speech. Emerging in a period of great educational and religious revival, the College needed to train ministers for a revived Church and a more highly educated public, to provide preachers for both the vast masses of the East End of London and for those pulpits where scholarship, as well as piety, was required.

Financial Strategy

The great majority of Anglican clergy of the time were drawn from wealthy and comfortable homes and had the means to pay for their own education. The main appeal of Non-conformists was also 'to the rising and growingly prosperous middle class.'[22] The future work for students of Spurgeon's College, however, lay among 'the working population, the real sinew and blood and bone of England'[23] and they needed to be men 'among men, practical, working, thoughtful.'

Spurgeon determined 'never to refuse a man on account of absolute poverty but rather to provide him with all needful food, board and raiment, that he might not be hindered on account of money'.[24] Only when relatives and friends could genuinely afford to make a subscription was this desired. Students were encouraged to buy their own books through the availability of cheap editions. The temptation was resisted to refuse poor men for the sake of the College's prestige and in favour of 'a better class of man'.[25] It was proved that 'eminently useful men' spring from all ranks and so the College would continue to aid the needy but pious brother who came from the class of ploughman, fisherman, and mechanic. In the early days of the College 'some very successful brethren needed everything, and if they had been required to pay they must have remained illiterate preachers.' This made early college finances precarious but, as the years went by, more and more men could support themselves in part or in whole.

The financial burden of the College rested initially, and continued to do so, upon Spurgeon's shoulders. At the outset, two of his deacons, Messrs. Winser and Olney, promised aid; but it was Spurgeon's own thrift and the donation of all proceeds from the sale of sermons to America, that substantially raised the £800 needed annually to support the students until 1861. During the slavery controversy his sermons ceased to sell in the United States and his income diminished. Several anonymous donors sent gifts of £100 or more to maintain the work but the regular income was now accepted as a responsibility of the Tabernacle congregations and they donated a weekly offering, which by 1869 provided £1,869 per year. 'How is the College supported?' Spurgeon was asked, and could confidently reply:

> The provision for the young men embraces everything which is necessary for their support—in some instances even to clothing and pin money. Their daily lives are under pastoral supervision. The weekly offerings in the Tabernacle, amounting to an average of more than £30 every Sabbath, are devoted exclusively to their support. All around the Tabernacle are placards inviting offerings and to those are attached notices of the amounts contributed on the last previous Sabbath.... 'To me this method has had special significance as a reminder that the raising up of them to preach the gospel is the first duty of the church.'[26]

A deacon, Mr Murrell, made the offering his special interest and ensured that any donations in excess of need were used for chapel building. Another deacon, Mr Phillips, gave an annual dinner to friends of the College to raise money.

The President's financial principles were greatly influenced by George Muller of Bristol, the Brethren preacher and founder of seven orphanages. Funds were to be sought through faith and prayer[27] after the style of the seventeenth-century German pietist, A.H. Francke. At the laying of the foundation stone at the Metropolitan Tabernacle on 16 August 1859, Spurgeon claimed that he had asked scarcely an individual for a contribution towards the building costs, 'because I have such a solid conviction that the money must come'.[28] In 1863 he criticised the Baptist Missionary Society for running into debt. By October 1864 he had made the acquaintance of James Hudson Taylor, the missionary pioneer to China, and in later years enjoyed his company on holiday in Mentone.[29] He adopted Taylor's motto, 'God's work done in God's way will never lack God's supply', for the College's financial policy. Ministerial training was under the 'faith-mission' principle.

Theological Priorities

The college was founded in stirring times, when traditional beliefs were feeling the shock of evolutionary ideas. Economic views popularised by Charles Kingsley (1819–1875), the English novelist and Christian socialist, and John Ruskin (1819–1900), the Victorian author and critic, were filtering through the minds of intelligent working men. The Anglo-Catholic movement filled ultra-Protestants with alarm. Spurgeon became very unhappy with contemporary trends in theology.[30] He claimed that 'Too many ministers are toying with the deadly Cobra of "another gospel", in the form of "modern thought".'[31] What was this 'modern thought', or this 'new theology' which Spurgeon called upon all true evangelicals to denounce as blasphemy against the Holy God?

Friedrich Schleiermacher (1768-1834), the German theologian, had advanced the belief that religion was not something which came from without, the impartation of a gift, but an eternal part of man's nature. This introduction of 'natural religion' stressed the instinctive religious inclinations of man. Hegel had attempted to unify Christianity and philosophy, and Strauss boldly tried to replace Christianity with philosophical truth. Bruno Bauer reduced the historical Christ to a product of the primitive Church, and Feuerbach concluded that religion originated in man's own thinking. Albert Ritschl, in his subjective idea of the Atonement, taught that men could not enter into full fellowship with the spirit of Christ until their sense of guilt was removed. The work of Christ was for this purpose. He denied that there was such a thing as true guilt and adhered to the belief that Christ's death removed this illusion.

During the nineteenth century these philosophical and theological ideas from Germany began to penetrate English thinking. Modern theological thought, however, began in England with Samuel Taylor Coleridge (1772-1834). His philosophy was more anthropocentric than theocentric. He taught that because of the mysterious character of the Atonement, its reasons and nature were incomprehensible. This important doctrine became a focal point for reinterpretation.

Dr William Magee of Ireland boldly stated that it was impossible to know how the death of Christ made possible the forgiveness of sins. He denied the efficacy of Christ's sacrifice and intercession. Along with others he spoke of the Atonement as an 'expedient', while another group thought of it as 'transcendent'.

Dr John McLeod Campbell (1800–1882), the Scottish theologian, denied the penal element in Christ's sufferings and advanced the theory that Christ, in his death, had made 'a perfect confession of our sins'.[32] 'This confession, as to its own nature,' he said, 'must have been a perfect Amen in humanity to the judgement of God on the sin of man.' It was further stated by Dr Campbell that 'he who would intercede for us must begin with confessing our sins.'

In his *Theological Essays*, and his book on *The Doctrine of Sacrifice*, F.D. Maurice (1805–1872), Christian socialist and teacher at King's College, London, stressed self-surrender as the vital element of Christ's death. His essential thought was that Christ simply manifested to men what God in his love had already achieved for mankind. Christ in his Atonement removed the moral anger of God, and therefore men have already been forgiven. Maurice denied the penal sufferings of Christ and stated that in his death Christ did not satisfy God. He believed in universal salvation, maintaining that all men were sons of God by creation, and children of God through Christ, defending his position by saying that God reconciled himself to men in Christ. 'Is not the Cross the meeting-point between man and man, between man and God?'[33]

Edward Pusey (1800–1882), leader of the Oxford Movement, argued against the necessity of Christ's death and held that the Incarnation was not absolutely necessary in freeing men from sin. His encouragement of ritualistic tendencies in the Church of England was also opposed by Spurgeon. More radical thinkers attacked the miraculous elements in the Christian faith.

T.H. Green, the Oxford philosopher of the Idealist School, regarded the miracles as impossibilities and confined Christ to the ordinary limitations of man. He confined faith in God to moral and intellectual standards.

Matthew Arnold (1822–1888), the English poet, with his philosophical agnosticism, ruled out orthodox belief in the supernatural element in religion and advocated an ethical idealism which placed God on an impersonal basis. 'The undoubted tendency of liberal opinion is to reject the whole anthropomorphic and miraculous religion of tradition, as unsound and untenable.'[34] Herbert Spencer, who held that God could not be known, may be placed in this same category.

Within the community of faith the nature of biblical inspiration and interpretation was carefully discussed. The fruit of this debate was particularly applied to the doctrine of hell.

F.W. Farrar (1831–1903), Dean of Canterbury, doubted the doctrine of eternal punishment, postulating that should there be a hell it would not be of literal fire.

> ...there are four elements in the current opinion which I consider to be as unsupported by Scripture as they are repugnant to reason.... These four elements...are (1) the physical torments, the material agonies, the 'sapiens ignis' of Eternal Punishment; (2) the supposition of its necessarily endless duration for all who incur it; (3) the opinion that it is incurred by the vast majority of mankind; and (4) that it is a doom passed irreversibly at the moment of death on all who die in a state of sin.[35]

In the face of all this new theology, Spurgeon declared

that he would continue to preach 'the old-fashioned doctrine'. 'I stand to the truth of the atonement though the Church is being buried beneath the boiling mud-showers of modern heresy.'[36] Horton Davies said, 'Spurgeon swam strongly against the tide of the age.'[37] Commenting that the critics did not think 'the boy preacher of Cambridgeshire'[38] would have staying power, he says 'they had forgotten the Calvinistic tradition in which he was reared.'[39] Spurgeon acknowledged freely his own debt to the Puritan divines.[40] If Spurgeon had a hero it was the unyielding Calvinist George Whitefield.[41] In 1871 he wrote:

> We say distinctly that the theology of the Pastors' College is Puritanic. The improvements brought forth by what is called 'modern thought' we regard with suspicion...we are old-fashioned enough to prefer Manton to Maurice, Charnock to Robertson and Owen to Voysey.[42]

Students preached acceptably among the Presbyterians in Scotland and Holland, yet Spurgeon's brand of Calvinism was 'illogical'.[43] He could declare the majesty of God and the freedom of man. He was dubbed an Arminian by high-Calvinist Baptists who disliked his open-communion views and the note of gospel invitation in his preaching. He defended zealously the doctrines of substitutionary atonement and everlasting punishment, and he maintained belief in an infallible Bible and verbal inspiration.

Spurgeon offered basically four arguments in defence of his conservative views. First, the validity of his faith was proven by his own experience. Second, his theology was that of the Puritans and represented the best traditions of the English religious experience. Third, in sharp contrast to the honest English manliness of his faith, the teachers of modern thought were offering an effeminate, watered-down gospel, foreign in its very origins. Finally his views, expressed in simple and dogmatic terms, were easily comprehended by those willing to make the leap across logic to faith. Such a conservative theological approach was linked to a strong educational principle.

Spurgeon's formal education had ended at secondary level and he had no advanced training in theology. He knew only two subjects thoroughly—the text of the English Bible and the writings of the Puritan divines. He eventually assembled one of the largest private collections of Puritan editions in the country.[44] He wanted to share his knowledge with those whose social class meant limited educational opportunities and financial privation.

The first Principal, George Rogers, shared his views. He had no sympathy with 'any modern concealment or perversion of great gospel truths.'[45] He loathed 'all mystic and rationalistic obscurations of the plain and full-orbed doctrines of grace', and explained that modernistic views were taught at the College only to be able to 'defend the things which are most surely believed among us.' Whilst acknowledging that ministers must know the errors of their day in order to meet them, a particular method of teaching was insisted upon intended to inculcate conviction not hesitation. Spurgeon maintained that tutors should not teach their students in that broad liberal manner which presents a number of viewpoints and leaves the ultimate choice to the student; rather they should forcibly and unmistakably declare the mind of God and show a determined predilection for the old theology, being saturated in it and ready to die for it.[46] Otherwise faith could be crippled, spiritual ardour dampened and morals corrupted in testing the theories of the hour.

This placed heavy responsibilities upon the tutors, since heresy in college would mean false teaching throughout the churches. To defile the fountain is to pollute the stream. Spurgeon pointed to the influence of Emmanuel College, Cambridge, in producing Puritan preachers for the Commonwealth period:

> The noblest school of English theologians sprang from the labours of tutors whose theology was sound and scriptural and whose learning was consecrated to the understanding of sacred writ. Had there been no such Puritan College there might have been no Puritan divines.[47]

Conversely he used Philip Doddridge's Evangelical Academy at Northampton as a warning against undogmatic preaching. 'Dr Doddridge was as sound as he was amiable, but perhaps he was not always judicious and not sufficiently bold and decided.' His successor, Dr Ashworth, continued the teaching policy—described by his pupil, Joseph Priestley, the Unitarian, in these words: 'In my time the academy was in a state peculiarly favourable to the serious pursuit of truth, as the students were about equally divided upon every question of much importance. Our tutors also were of different opinions...the general plan of our studies...was exceedingly favourable to free enquiry, as we were referred to authors on both sides of every question.'[48]

If ignorance was never an aid to grace, then learning must be dominated by 'the doctrine of grace coupled with a firm belief in human responsibility—held with intense conviction.'[49]

In an article in *The Times* of 13 April 1857, strong doctrine was linked with sound preaching.

> Eloquence that will move the masses requires not merely a loud voice but proper material to exert itself upon... there must be a strong sentiment, some bold truth to make a man shout. The doctrine of sudden conversion or of irresistible grace can be shouted.[50]

Agreeing with such sentiment, tutors at the College were required to be both dogmatic and fervent. 'They should thunder in preaching, and lighten in conversation, they should be flaming in prayer, shining in life and burning in spirit.... The spirit of the gospel must be in him as well as its doctrine.'[51]

As one examines Spurgeon's commitment to education, it is clear that he was a principled man, reflecting the voluntaryist inheritance of the denomination in which he ministered, yet pragmatic in his outlook to State schooling, and in the provision of college finances. He was not afraid to advertise the needs of the College, and to enlist all kinds of people and means in fund-raising activities. He may have taken his financial principles from others, but he certainly went further in hammering them out on the anvil of experience. He was committed to firm theological and educational principles, but always wanted to relate these to the people that God actually set around him. He wanted to stretch each man according to his ability, so was prepared to train those whose earlier educational opportunities were very limited, whilst financing others towards university education. He was idealistic, flexible and practical in his approach.

The staff of dissenting colleges in the nineteenth century

always faced the danger of becoming rigid, and teaching a static theology. Many came from narrow homes and agrarian backgrounds, and possessed little experience of industrial life. At Spurgeon's College, pastoral experience was common among tutors and the College was linked to a local church. Yet academic qualifications were moderate and longevity of service exposed tutors to the danger of diminishing effectiveness. Staff leadership lay in the hands of President and Principal.

Spurgeon's principles and personality influenced every area of college life, but his Friday afternoon lectures to the students on ministerial life and practice were the main occasions when his gifts were indelibly marked upon the characters of the students. He said:

> I am as much at home with my young brethren as in the bosom of my family and therefore speak without restraint...I have purposely given an almost autobiographical tinge to the whole, because my own experience, such as it is, is the most original contribution which I can offer, and with my own students, quite as weighty as any other within my reach.[52]

Whilst Spurgeon did little formal lecturing, his role as President meant that he was the spiritual mentor and model for the students. He interviewed them before they were accepted for training at the College, superintended their settlement procedure, often acted as financial adviser and support for their young growing churches, and continued voluminous correspondence with many of the students once they were out in the pastorate.

The day-to-day administration of the College was in the hands of his brother, James Spurgeon, and the Principals,

Fig. 1.4 Rev. Charles Haddon Spurgeon, the founder and first President of the College 1856–1892.

Rogers and then Gracey. But because the Pastors' College was linked with the Tabernacle Church in a way that was unique, C.H. Spurgeon became the model pastor, whose preaching eloquence, theological position and spiritual stature the students sought to emulate. His influence in word and deed upon nearly half a century of Baptist ministers was profound. The Pastors' College was named, not primarily to describe its function, but as a tribute to the Founder's influence.

John Clifford said: 'His is the most pronounced Baptist force of the last quarter of a century. His works are as abundant as his position is unique.'[53] He felt Spurgeon possessed Whitefield's passion for saving souls and the practical organising skill of Wesley. Dr E.A. Payne claimed: 'He was recognised as unquestionably the greatest preacher in an age of great preachers.'[54] Helmut Thielicke recorded the way his sermons were cabled to New York and reprinted in the newspapers of the country every Monday morning.[55] Horton Davies discusses his preaching critically: 'On the debit side must be set cultural and even theological Philistinism: a frequently eccentric exposition of Holy Writ and a maudlin sentimentality. His sermons lack profoundity, erudition and elegance.'[56] Yet he declares: 'Apart from the Calvinistic certainties welcomed by his unsophisticated and conservative hearers, it was the enthusiasm, the manly directness, the racy vigour of his phrasing, the clarity and order of his planning and the variety and aptness of his illustrations and references that accounted for his widespread appeal. His sermons have vigour, relevance and interest.' E.A. Payne mentions his humour, pungency and matchless voice: A.C. Underwood his directness and realism which 'marked him off at once from his immediate predecessors in London pulpits'.[57]

Spurgeon was largely a self-taught man who, but for a misunderstanding about the meeting plans for an interview, might have trained at the Stepney Academy.[58] His mind was independent and his words often outspoken. He made his mark at a time of great preachers and in the day of the Second Religious Revival. His life was free from cant and guile; he was devoid of self-seeking and had a vital and rich personal religious experience. These things gave him an influence that has continued long after the personalities of most of his contemporaries have become dim.'[59]

The College was his most cherished creation. Its idea, formulation and support were his chief concern. He said, 'By that I multiply myself...it is my first-born and best beloved.'[60] He exercised self-denial in order that the work might be maintained, giving a substantial part of his income to its upkeep. He justified his project on the grounds of 'the altered state of society'[61] and those characteristics which the Pastors' College 'has in distinction' from other London colleges.

Three factors account for the successful ministry of Spurgeon. First he recognised the Holy Spirit as a distinct Person, and not an emanation from God. He referred to the Spirit as the 'key' and the 'Private Tutor' through whom all spiritual enlightenment came. If Spurgeon were living today he would denounce those biographers who claim that his success was largely due to his heredity, or to his golden voice, or to his unique personality. In his characteristic way he would declare that his power and success came by the Holy Spirit who brought the 'effectual blow' of 'irresistible grace' to his heart. In his *Lectures to My Students*, Spurgeon said, 'Our hope of success, and our strength for continuing the service, lie in our belief that the Spirit of the Lord resteth upon us.'[62]

The second factor contributing to Spurgeon's success may be stated in three words: love for Christ. He said, 'the test is this, the loving of Christ' and added that this 'can only be ascribed to faith.'[63]

The third factor, which Spurgeon himself gave as the reason for his success, was that his preaching was Christ-centred. He stated that 'The best way to reach sinners for Christ is to preach Christ to sinners.'[64] His love for Christ resulted in a Christ-centred ministry. His motto was 'Jesus only'. He never magnified himself. He gave himself unreservedly to Christ, and with a child-like faith implicitly trusted in the promises which God had extended through Christ. He said, 'I resolve, God helping me, in my preaching to preach to you nothing else save Jesus Christ.'[65]

Spurgeon's own character and experience were formative for his college. He was not immune from adversity, suffering himself from physical affliction and mental anguish. The Church too was not free from the pain of corporate distress, especially in the wake of cholera and fire damage. God, in his sovereign wisdom, does not exempt the Christian from the tunnels of doubt, suffering and difficulty, but rather refines the character of the individual through those experiences so that the ministry may have a depth, sensitivity, compassion and dimension that would otherwise have been impossible.

Spurgeon was committed to the gospel of the Lord Jesus Christ and his saving power. At the heart of all his enterprise and of all his preaching, Spurgeon was Christocentric and soteriological. In this respect Spurgeon was a typical evangelical, committed to the Bible, the Cross, conversion and resulting activism. His was a gospel ministry and he was a gospel preacher.

He had an experiential faith. In his ministry he saw God at work, he saw lives transformed, he witnessed prayers answered, he knew the reality of a God who was transcendently sovereign and therefore to be trusted, yet was imminently near and to be known in the events of daily life.

A man of clear convictions, Spurgeon was prepared to see them challenged without wavering, to see them criticised without shifting and to see them proclaimed with earnestness and eloquence. He forged his convictions at an early stage in his life and maintained them to the end. He was a man of hard work and deep commitment. Although he had a very great natural preaching gift, he fostered and developed it through practice, through reading, through study, through careful thought and earnest prayer. Though he developed an effective ministry through his preaching gift, he did not neglect, particularly in the early years of his ministry in London, the hard slog of regular pastoral visitation, of getting to know people's names, of being in their homes and inviting them to his home. When students were in the College he did not simply teach them, he was available to them as their counsellor and guide. When they came to finish their courses he was available to them as the Governor who sent them out to needy areas to begin Christian work. When they were in that work he organised gatherings to inspire and encourage them. He wrote to them, he earned money for them, he was with them.

Spurgeon's home-life matched his public life. In him there was no guile, only sincerity. What he was at home, at church and at work, was consistently the same. He was, with his friends and his enemies, a man in Christ. His home-life was known. There were frequent visitors. There was real partnership in his marriage. His sons came to baptism.

Further reflection can also lead to a more critical analysis. It could be said that Spurgeon dominated his enterprises to the point where he may have curtailed the development and activity of others, and he made insufficient plans for the future of his institutions beyond his death. Certainly the Tabernacle went through a very difficult four-year period trying to decide who should succeed him, and the College found that within three years of his death, radical changes had to be made to its syllabus, its intake and its financial position.

It could be said that Spurgeon's theology in 1892 was exactly what it was when he was converted. Not being a college man himself and largely self-taught, he maintained, not only in content but in expression, the Puritan theology which he had inherited through parental influence and private reading. This limited his theological relevance to future evangelicalism.

It could be said that Spurgeon had a limited discernment of people. He was so warm-hearted, concerned and helpful that sometimes people were able to take advantage of his generosity. He was not always able to administer personal rebuke. Nevertheless he generated in those around him a loyalty, respect and faithfulness and was held in awe by all who knew him.

In his training of other leaders he was keen to train pastor/evangelists who were able to convert people, to save souls and to start churches. He was not quite as good at training the pastor/teacher who was able, with conviction and

Fig. 1.5 A score from C.H. Spurgeon's Friday afternoon pastoral lectures to the students.

continuity, to preach the Word of God every Sunday in such a way that the saints were built up, churches matured and Christians sanctified.

Finally, it is probably true that although in the major years of his life and ministry he engaged in rich evangelical fellowship across denominational barriers and within his own denomination, he did in the end become a separatist.

Today his memory is cherished by many who stand in the separatist and evangelical tradition and he is especially popular in what was the Underground Church in Eastern Europe, in the Southern Baptist Convention in the United States and in the Reformed Church in Great Britain. There is no doubt that at the end of his life, on doctrinal grounds, he adopted that separatist position. His influence in the wider Baptist family suffered when he left that denomination, although it has continued amongst British Baptists through institutions that bear his name. Nevertheless Spurgeon was committed to Kingdom life which held the balance between evangelism and social action in holistic mission which has a contemporary ring. He remains a figure of considerable importance.

CHAPTER 2

The Institution
1856–1892

Principals

THE MAIN BURDEN OF TEACHING fell in the early years to George Rogers, the Principal. Although an uncompromising paedobaptist, Rogers was catholic-minded, witty and judicious and he shared Spurgeon's enthusiasm for Calvinistic doctrine. He was born in 1799 into a large Nonconformist family in Essex. Educated at Rotherham Academy (1819–21), he ministered briefly at Hulme, Manchester, and then as an assistant to John Clayton at the Weigh House Chapel, London. Later he was pastor at Upminister and then ministered with great distinction in Camberwell (1829–65), whilst acquiring a thorough academic and theological knowledge.[1] His home was the base for college studies in the first five years when fifteen students began their course—seven from Southwark, and eight from the provinces. Classes were conducted in the style of a late seventeenth-century academy. Rogers served as Principal until 1881 and was remembered as 'grim, gaunt, grey'[2] by his students, although he acted as a fatherly figure towards them as well as a theological teacher.

In the early days he was assisted by men in full-time pastoral ministry. James Cubitt, whose main charge was at

Thrapston, and J.W. Genders, of Wandsworth, both taught the students.[3] Lecturers, such as B. Davies, W.R. Selway, D.C. Evans and W. Durban, taught both ministerial candidates and evening class students. Once the College moved to premises at the Metropolitan Tabernacle in 1862, the teaching was mainly in the hands of two men—David Gracey, whose 'influence upon his students cannot be measured',[4] and Archibald Fergusson, who taught English.

H.O. Mackey says of Rogers: 'All his previous training and mental habits had been getting him ready for this lifework.'[5] He had continued to study assiduously while in pastorates, preparing himself to be a capable teacher of others. Writing after ten years' friendship, Spurgeon said, 'Mr Rogers is a man of Puritan stamp, deeply learned, orthodox in doctrine, devout, earnest, liberal in spirit and withal juvenile in heart to an extent most remarkable in one of his years.'[6] Many students never forgot his ordination addresses, in which he set before them the ideals of ministry. His upright, venerable figure, the measured tone of his speech, the lurking humour, all made for a formidable influence as he appealed for prayerful support in the new ministry.

Rogers delivered lectures on systematic theology each Wednesday morning in college. They were characterised by doctrinal instruction, scriptural proof and logical presentation. After a bewildering variety of criticism from fellow students, a few racy sentences of pithy description from the Principal would sum up the sermon class. Some remembered his verdicts for their courteous but crushing condemnations; others for their balanced but helpful appreciations; all for their keen insight. He also made a rich contribution in addresses to the annual Conferences of former students.

He laid down some of his responsibilities in 1881 and retired completely from the work of the College in 1884, dying in 1892, the same year as Spurgeon. Both came from Essex and although Spurgeon was only twenty-three and Rogers nearly sixty years old when they came together to begin Spurgeon's College, their friendship was firm, cemented by a common doctrinal commitment.

In 1881 David Gracey assumed the Principalship and F.G. Marchant came to assist in teaching science. Gracey was born in Co. Down in 1841 into a Presbyterian family. He began to work for a firm of grain importers, but developed a sense of call to the ministry, and soon entered Glasgow University in 1859 with a view to that end. During his short stay in Glasgow University he acted as a city missioner there, but on learning that students and staff at Pastors' College disapproved of University qualifications in a Baptist minister, he abandoned his studies. On the same basis many years later he declined several offers of honorary degrees. After hearing Spurgeon preach in Glasgow in 1861, Gracey applied for admission to Pastors' College.

He appears to have entered the College in a dual role. At first he was considered one of the students but then began to help out with tutoring. Two or three months after his admission, Mr Cubitt was forced to retire and David Gracey became Classical Tutor. He had never exercised pastoral charge, but between 1873 and 1886 he preached regularly for the church at New Southgate. He remained Classical Tutor until 1881, when he became Principal, a post he held until his death in February 1893, aged fifty-two. At the College Conference it was said of him, 'To a succession of more than 800 students he brought scholarship of no mean power, a character beautiful as it was modest... a loyalty to God and truth which eminently fitted him to guide others, and a patience beyond praise...'[7] Colleagues recalled his courtesy and graciousness, coupled with industry, acumen and perseverance which would have enabled him to succeed in the commercial world.

His self-forgetfulness exposed him to daily visitors whose passing needs could overburden him, but it was his gifts and work as a teacher that most won admiration. Orderly in his methods, exact in his observation, he was a skilful dialectician and possessed vast information on almost all subjects that ever came under discussion. His lovable disposition, devout and deep faith, his whole-hearted consecration enhanced the quality of his work. Former students who resided with the Gracey family recalled his calm temperament and his charm, which won and held their affections. Ever approachable, he sympathised patiently, listened carefully, and offered gentle but confident advice. His commercial experience complemented Rogers' pastoral experience; his youth enlivened Rogers' maturity. Gracey and Rogers took little part in denominational affairs: they taught the students. Charles Haddon Spurgeon and his brother James Archer Spurgeon represented the college to the wider world.

In contrast to the intellectual emphasis, educational experience and career pattern that characterised Anglican theological colleges, the staff at Pastors' College displayed a haphazard career development. Tutors generally remained in their job until death or retirement. Most had one or more pastorates before they became tutors, and some combined a pastorate with tutoring. Very few of the tutors engaged in a writing ministry. For most of them however it was important that they could speak eloquently and teach winsomely the doctrines of Grace.

Tutors

Some of the earliest tuition was undertaken by local ministers, whose time at the College was thus limited. John Genders[8] was of Huguenot origin and received a grammar school education. Brought up in the Established Church, he heard Spurgeon preach in London, was baptised and became one of the first students at Pastors' College. On leaving, he first went as a tutor to schools in Weston-super-Mare and Bath, but Spurgeon recalled him to teach Hebrew and Greek at Pastors' College. While doing so, he was minister at East Hill, Wandsworth, where a new church was built under his leadership. He subsequently ministered at Luton, Portsea and Ilfracombe, but retired from pastoral office at the age of fifty-five to devote himself to writing and translation work.

James Cubitt[9] grew up in rural Suffolk and from his earliest days took part in Sunday school teaching and village preaching. At twenty-one he began to study for the ministry under the oversight of W. Hawkins of Derby, and finished his ministerial training at Stepney College in 1834. After twenty-six years of pastoral ministry, he taught Classics at the Pastors' College for two years.

George Rogers was not the only Congregationalist on the staff of the College. A colleague, William Robbins Selway,[10] served as science lecturer at Pastors' College. Although a layman, he reflected Congregational principles and a paedobaptist point of view. He was a surveyor who served on the Metropolitan Board of Works. The main teaching in the nineteenth century was, however, done by three long-serving tutors who were Baptist ministers. They typified the pastoral connection and longevity of service which gave stability and continuity to the teaching work at Spurgeon's College. Frederick Marchant[11] was born at Brabourne in Kent in 1839 into a churchwarden's family, but was baptised and received into the Baptist church as the age of sixteen. Not content with the education then given to farmers' sons, he studied at home and engaged in local preaching. He later became one of Spurgeon's earliest students and had his first church in Lodge Lane, Birmingham, where he stayed six years. He had two further pastorates, at Wandsworth and Hitchin, before becoming, at Spurgeon's request, classical and mathematical tutor at Pastors' College in 1879. After serving eighteen years in that capacity, when Gracey died, Marchant became acting Principal and theological lecturer. He had retained the pastoral oversight of the Hitchin church and about that time he was also engaged in writing a commentary on Joshua. In 1887, following the death of his wife and the increasing ill health of his daughter, he gave up the pastorate in Hitchin, retaining only his tutorship. By 1898 his own ill health was hindering his work at Spurgeon's College, yet he was still nominally serving there when he died in 1899.

Archibald Fergusson[12] was born in Scotland in 1821 and converted at Dundee in 1839. Nothing is known of his early life, but he came to London about 1860 to take up a post as evening tutor in Pastors' College. Six months later he became one of the regular tutors, while retaining the evening class responsibility. He directed the English department which was a painstaking responsibility because most students had received only limited education but needed to communicate

Fig. 2.1 The Rev. James Archer Spurgeon, DD, LL.D, the second President of the College 1892–1896.

effectively. Although hard-worked at the College, he planted a Baptist cause at Ealing, meeting at first in a barn behind a public house. Eventually a new Baptist chapel was opened and Fergusson ministered there for twenty-eight years, alongside his tutorship. He published his only book while at the height of these activities, in 1870, called *Particular Redemption and the Universal Gospel Offer*. He died at the age of seventy-nine.

James Archer Spurgeon,[13] younger brother of the founder, was born in Braintree in 1837. He undertook four years' commercial work on leaving school. At the age of nineteen he entered Stepney College to train for the Baptist ministry. Although impressed and influenced by the gifts and spirituality of his brother Charles, he was able to attract crowded congregations in his own right, and accepted the invitation, instigated by Alexander McLaren, to the pastorate of Portland Chapel, Southampton, when he was twenty-two. The numbers he attracted soon necessitated the enlargement of the building. In this first year of ministry he took part in the stone-laying ceremony at the Metropolitan Tabernacle.

From Portland he moved to found the Chapel at Carlton, Southampton, in spite of invitations to Bristol and to succeed his brother at New Park Street, which continued separately after the opening of the Tabernacle. In 1863 however, James came to London as first minister of the new chapel in Cornwall Road, Bayswater. From this time he was associated with his brother's projects, culminating in his acceptance of the co-pastorate of the Tabernacle in 1868, when he was thirty-one years old.

In addition to the oversight of the growing work at Bayswater, he became Vice-President of the College and secretary to the College Evangelical Association, formed in 1865. He contributed articles to *The Sword and the Trowel* and from 1866 found time to lecture at the College two days a week on a wide variety of subjects. He travelled throughout the country, and was a most acceptable substitute preacher at the Tabernacle when his brother was absent.

The Tabernacle became a vast concern and the business side was a constant source of anxiety. In 1867 Charles Spurgeon became desperately ill and this brought home to his deacons the urgent need to relieve him of the cares of

Fig. 2.2 Former Presidents and tutors of the Old Pastors' College.

administration. Their thoughts turned to his brother who was already giving him valuable assistance. James received an unanimous invitation to become co-pastor. This delicate position could only be occupied by a man willing to forego his own independence for the greater good: this James did out of love for his brother and a deep concern to forward the work of God. He only occupied the Tabernacle pulpit when Charles was indisposed, though then sometimes at short notice, but as a preacher he was much in demand. A year after he became co-pastor he also took charge of a small cause at West Croydon, where the twenty-nine members who had called him grew to 441 by the time of his death.

Always slightly overshadowed by his elder brother,

James was himself an outstanding minister and wielded great influence. He served as President of the London Baptist Association, toured the USA and Canada, and exercised a fruitful evangelistic ministry. He was a sound Hebrew scholar, a fine teacher and a consistent but tactful Baptist. He died while Vice-President of the Baptist Union in 1900.

It would be foolish to denigrate the business acumen, theological commitment and academic ability of the staff of Spurgeon's College. Nevertheless, the organisation and the apportioning of teaching responsibility was modelled on the seventeenth and eighteenth-century academy model without that development in educational organisation and intellectual advance which characterised New College, where Congregational ministers were trained, in the nineteenth-century. Spurgeon's offered a practical training, undertaken by many men whose educational advantages were slim. Such people needed meticulous tuition, a great deal of personal care and the development of practical skills for a pioneering and church-planting ministry. The staff were personally selected and appointed by Spurgeon to meet those needs.

Students

C.H. Spurgeon elucidated the principles behind the choice of his students. He was able personally to select those who conformed to his ideals: 'The men whom God must honour will be gracious men, full of the Holy Spirit, called of God to their work, anointed, qualified and divinely sustained.'[14] They would exhibit plain speech, sound doctrine, common sense, humility, popular sympathy, a single-mindedness to save souls, self-sacrifice and dogged resolution: such a striking spiritual model had a profound effect on the conception of ministry among nineteenth-century Baptists.

This followed the views of eighteenth-century evangelicals such as Philip Doddridge and earlier Puritan leaders, such as Perkins and Baxter. They pointed to five standards in the examination of a candidate for the ministry: the authenticity of his religious experience, the acceptability of his moral character, the genuineness of his call, the correctness of his doctrine, and the adequacy of his preparation.

In order to gain such men, Spurgeon cast his net as widely as possible, giving access to all men truly called of God and of proven ability in preaching. They would be trained in a spiritual atmosphere at a church-based college by tutors of Puritan theology to the academic level each could attain.

In 1856 there were seven Baptist training colleges in Britain. Talk of rationalisation was in the air. Yet in that year C.H. Spurgeon began a further institution for the benefit of one initial student. First hearing Spurgeon speak at a Sunday School Anniversary meeting, Medhurst was convinced of sin.[15] He wrote to Spurgeon: 'Do, dear Sir, tell me how I can find Jesus.'[16] A number of letters were exchanged. Medhurst was converted and interviewed for baptism and church membership. Spurgeon recorded in his notebook: 'A very promising young man—his letters to me evince various degrees of progress in the pilgrim's road.'

Medhurst continues the story:

> 'I at once began to preach in the open air and elsewhere, though I had not then any idea of entering the ministry. Two persons who became members at New Park Street through my preaching led Mr Spurgeon to suggest that I should prepare myself for pastoral

work. Arrangements were made for me in July 1855 to go to reside with the Rev. C.H. Hosken at Crayford.'

In 1856 he was invited to become pastor at Kingston-upon-Thames and this was undertaken part-time until two years' training was completed. He went to reside with Rev. George Rogers on 21 March 1857, and a little later a second student, E.J. Silverton, was received. Medhurst went on to pastor churches in England, Ireland and Scotland for forty years, concluding with a period of service at Hope Baptist Chapel, Canton, Cardiff.

In 1862 forty-six students were accepted for training when accommodation at the Metropolitan Tabernacle had replaced the cramped conditions at the Camberwell Manse. These included two converted Jews who went to work among their own people[17] and a Primitive Methodist who returned after a year's course to work in the circuit in North London. Each student received fifteen shillings a week and the men were boarded in twos and threes in the houses of Tabernacle families. This unusual method of lodging was preferred to community living because it kept the students in touch with family life, problems and finances, and meant that they were not elevated above the social position which in all probability they would have to occupy in succeeding years.

The selection of candidates for admission was principally determined by evidence of spirituality, a teachable spirit, great zeal for the salvation of souls and some evidence of effectiveness in Christian work. There was no entrance examination to the College. As a third of all students came from the Tabernacle, testimony to character and achievement was not difficult to obtain. Great stress was always laid on the role of the sending church and great value attached to the references provided by those who knew the candidate best.

Initial applications were made to the lay secretary. Testimonials often accompanied applications emphasising experience, devotion, gift and evangelistic commitment. The following extracts accompanied Mr Boyce's application in 1890:

> 'His aim has been to live the Christian life as well as preach it...worker...speaker...considerable ability.... His addresses have always been well received, and appreciated, and his grand ideal has always been the Cross. Jesus Christ and him crucified.... A burning love for the souls of his fellow creatures.... His addresses have always shown that they were well thought out, before being delivered, and they have been many a time blessed to souls...I know a case where he was instrumental in God's hands of leading a Roman Catholic to accept Jesus as his own Saviour...permeates with the love of Jesus.'[18]
>
> 'From the zeal and ability he has shown in connection with the work I have no doubt as to Mr Boyces' future success in the ministry of the gospel.... Earnest and intelligent he grasps the subject which he may take up in such a manner as to secure the attention of an audience which although of the most degraded class is not by any means less critical than a highly trained or cultivated one... Very brilliant future.'[19]
>
> 'Very hearty in spirit and devoted to mission work...good deal of fitness.... Direct gospel work would I think be his forte and to gain preparation for this is his aim in applying to the Pastors' College.... His word was enjoyed.... He has done and is doing some good work in connection with the Leith Young Men's Fellowship Union.'[20]
>
> 'Well qualified to preach the gospel of Christ and I do believe with the talents that God has given him he would be of great service to the church in the building up of saints and in the conversion of sinners.'[21]

'I feel convinced that he was specially gifted for the work, and likely to be used by God as a soulwinner, my impression of him has been fully realised, he has made a marked progress in the divine life... I am confident he will prove a great blessing.'[22]

'Pleasing presence and voice and style of address and from these natural gifts and from his warm interest in Christian work I think there is reason to hope that after training he would prove to be an acceptable and with God's blessing a successful preacher of the old and glorious gospel.'[23]

'An apt and forcible speaker, full of Christian zeal and of a devoted spirit... I feel confident that by the grace of God there is a bright and useful career before him.'[24]

'A young man of excellent parts.... He is robust in health.... He has a good voice.... He expresses himself well.... He is earnest and enthusiastic.... A useful minister of the Lord Jesus Christ.'[25]

'His moral character is unimpeachable.'[26]

Spurgeon interviewed candidates peronally and tried to put them off the ministry, emphasising its demands and poverty. Certainly he never tempted men into the College. Many prospective students were daunted by the need to have preached regularly for two years before entering college. Others were turned off by the long and tedious enquiries made before they were accepted. yet others were judged unfit for the ministry. Within the Baptist denomination such a refusal did not necessarily mean that a man could not be pastor of a church. There was no central ministerial recognition.[27]

Spurgeon was rigorous about the need for careful discrimination and refused to shrink from removing unsuitable students from the college course, because he felt that once

Fig. 2.3 C.H. Spurgeon with former students in 1888, including the first college student, Tom Medhurst, on the extreme right in the front row.

such men are in churches 'the grief is deeper because the mischief is not so readily remedied.'[28] He believed any called and gifted man's ministry would be enhanced through training: 'Divine truth loses none of its power by being spoken in correct English: neither will it be any the less clear if set forth by a person familiar with his Bible in its original tongue.'[29] This value was recognised even by men already in pastorates and so the age of students varied widely.[30]

The basic length of course was fixed at two years, lengthened to three years in 1880, but there was flexibility depending on academic ability and openings for service. Of those who entered in 1862, eighteen stayed one year, nineteen completed two years, three left in 1865 and six had to remain for four years. In the early years students were tempted away by churches before their courses were complete. Men entered their ministry prematurely and in a raw state. Deacons entreated them to take churches and thus save souls. Such leaders thought Spurgeon a 'harsh jailor' if he detained students when there was work to be done. But in the 80s there was a lull in demand from churches and men could stay for a third year, which was 'more useful than the other two.'[31]

Vacations were short,[32] giving an intensive course, brief enough not to cool the first ardour for the ministry and extensive enough to equip a man for further study and work in his later life. The numbers oscillated—seventeen came in 1863; forty in 1864; fourteen in 1865; twenty-five in 1866; thirty-seven in 1867. Overall numbers varied from ninety-three in 1868, seventy-eight in 1873, to a peak of one hundred and ten in 1877. These figures all related to training for full-time ministry and do not include those engaged in evening classes.[33]

The devotional life of students was encouraged by Spurgeon[34] and recognised in the Press.[35] Corporate prayers were held at the beginning and end of each day and there was a prayer meeting each week. The College Missionary Society and Temperance Society encouraged wide vision and self-control. The link with the Tabernacle gave the students the counsel of wise officers of the church and a familiarity with church discipline and organisation. It was claimed that the church created an atmosphere free from disagreement, envy, jealousy, adverse criticism and unhelpful frivolity.[36] James Spurgeon stresses the point: 'We have, therefore, kept ever in mind the strong necessity of our young brethren taking part in all our prayer meetings, occasionally attending our church meetings, constantly helping in our varied platform meetings and watching in general all our departments of work as now existing in the huge agglomeration of services and charities which encircle the Tabernacle as the centre of their influence and the mainspring of their order and power. Our recruits are drilled in the camp itself, and amidst all the exercises of actual and successful spiritual welfare... the successful operations of the Tabernacle church are a magnificent school for all students to work in and acquire the methods and precedents to quote and apply in coming years.' Spurgeon expected one distinguished minister from every eight students, but he could boastfully describe the work of most as 'perfectly marvellous' and 'exceedingly gratifying'.[37]

Curriculum

On Tuesday 9 August 1881 the students reassembled after the vacation, gathering in the grounds of Joseph Tritton's home in Upper Norwood. They engaged in a short devotional service, new students were introduced by Spurgeon, various outdoor amusements were enjoyed as a means of engaging friendships and the day ended with the hope: 'May this session be rich with benediction and the College do the best work it has ever yet accomplished.'[38] Educational ambition was not lacking. In the reports of each year's work there is inevitable repetition: 'The usual course of study has been steadily pursued for the past year with quite average results.'[39] Student progress was maintained with painstaking effort by long-serving professors teaching a stable curriculum.

The pastoral work of the main lecturers did not detract from the advance of the students. Mr Marchant held a pastorate at Hitchin, which made 'severe demands upon my time and strength' but he was 'much gratified by the general progress of the students in my classes.'[40] The work at Hitchin benefitted from his wider work: 'My congregations were never so good as they have been for the past three years; a spirit of unusual prayer and earnestness has animated the people; seventy persons nearly all from the world were last year added to the work.'[41]

Visiting lecturers came in times of need. For instance in 1889 when Spurgeon was away in Mentone, his practical lectures were given by David Davies of Brighton, Dr Sinclair Paterson and James Douglas; Mr Richardson came in regularly to give class teaching and individual instruction in the special skills of public speaking. The students were mainly surrounded by familiar faces and were taught according to clear principles. Spurgeon said, 'To all we labour to give a liberal English education and sound Biblical instruction.'[42] Rogers stressed that, unlike universities, the separation of 'secular and theological studies is not...one of the most hopeful signs of the times.'[43]

Spurgeon was clear about the balanced curriculum he desired:

1. A knowledge of the Scriptures, studying whole books and making the best use of commentaries, expositions and introductions.
2. The study of doctrine.
3. The history of the church and the history of the nation.
4. The rudiments of Astronomy, Chemistry, Zoology, Geology and Botany.

5. Mental and Moral Science, Metaphysics and Casuistry.
6. Mathematics.
7. Latin, Greek and Hebrew.
8. Composition and Style.
9. Poetry.
10. Practical Oratory.
11. The conduct of church work.[44]

This curriculum was designed to give men the education of which many were deprived in childhood and to enable them to proclaim the gospel with interest and relevance. Up to 1880 the weekly timetable of student study was substantially unchanged. Every man's progress was checked in classes with James Spurgeon on Mondays and Fridays by questions and written work. At the beginning of the week the junior students met the Vice-President to study Greek History and read short essays on topics such as the History and Dogmas of the Church of Rome and Mission Work. Reading and dictation exercises often ended these sessions.

The first hour and a half on a Wednesday was devoted to Systematic Theology, taught by the Principal. There exists a set of notes taken down in detail by one of the students during Gracey's lectures in the autumn term of 1879.[45] Eighteen lectures were recorded: five of an introductory character, ten on the doctrine of sin and three on salvation. The first lecture surveys the main heresies from Gnosticism to nineteenth-century scepticism: the student was taught to challenge deviant opinion.

Lectures two to four justify the arrangement, discussing the system by which the truths of revelation are connected, the method or principle by which truth is ascertained, and finally the order of those truths in a scriptural system. It is clear that the Bible is to be the only ground of authority: 'We go not to the pages of the Bible to underline, to erase or to add to what is written there but as disciples to learn their contents; not to put our ideas into it but to draw our ideas from it.'[46] After reviewing the systems of Augustine, Aquinas, Calvin and Doddridge, Gracey emphasises the Christocentric stress in the evangelistic preaching of Jonathan Edwards and Andrew Fuller. Finally, in lecture five he emphasises his aim in lecturing in this way—to make better preachers of the gospel and enhance personal devotion to Christ.

Lectures six to fifteen are on the familiar evangelical starting point of sin, covering its fact, its biblical expressions, its nature and definition; the requirements and the authority of the law, sin in man, the fall, the imputation of sin and the outlook for sinners. The lectures display orderliness and depth. Gracey gives four reasons for giving priority to the subject of sin,[47] and then expounds ten Hebrew and thirteen Greek words on the topic. The purpose in examining the biblical words in the original languages he says is to 'dispense as much as possible with speculation and to fill the mind with biblical truth before forming a theory, so that we may be better able to examine the theory.'[48]

In the lecture on the nature of sin Strauss is quoted scornfully: 'Human kind is impeccable for the progress of its development is irreproachable.'[49] Ten Protestant divines are quoted to define sin. Passages such as 1 John 3 and 4 on the subject of unrighteousness, and Romans 5 on the subject of Adam-Christ typology are expounded in detail. Dale's theory of antithesis, that we can conceive of law apart from God but not of God apart from law, is derided as 'darkening counsel by words without knowledge.'[50] Gracey adopts the theory of moral law that acknowledges two elements in law—intelligence referred to the divine understanding and binding force referred to the divine will. Extensive space is given to expounding the Calvinistic view of total depravity and the literal place of Adam in the spread of racial wickedness as the natural and legal head of the race. The lectures on sin end with a portrait of divine wrath and judgement, handled with brevity and sensitivity. All this is 'introductory and preparatory to the declarations of God's free mercy in Christ Jesus. Tis for the purpose of shutting men up to the hope of the gospel, not for the purpose of shutting them out.'[51]

Salvation is treated as hope, speculation, doctrine and mystery and its unfolding in history, language, imagery and experience are examined. Conservative writers, such as Chalmers and Trench, are quoted approvingly and the imagery of the material, social and legal world is explored fully. The concepts of ransom, reconciliation, justification and salvation are expounded and the penal substitutionary view of atonement is dogmatically asserted. One cannot be sure whether the lecture notes are complete. The section on salvation is rounded and conclusive, even if brief. The notes appear almost verbatim, achieved either by slow delivery, shorthand, or copied accounts. The last three lectures may have been abbreviated for the sake of completion at the end of the term; but the disparity between the number of lectures on sin and those on salvation may point to an unbalanced concentration on the negative aspect of doctrine. However, there is in the possession of the College a copy of 'Lectures given by Principal Gracey in the Pastors' College to the students in 1887–89.'[52] It appears that another student, Mr Morrison, took down about fourteen pages of notes per week. The topics—Depravity, Imputation of sin, and Salvation—were covered as they had been ten years earlier; but the course went further and prophetic insights into salvation were thoroughly explored under three headings:

1. The growth of variety in the course of prophecy.
2. The growth of the distinct personality of the Saviour.
3. The growth of the particulars of his life and death.

The person of Jesus was examined, affirming his true deity, true humanity and unity of two natures in one personality. Particular stress was laid on his deity, which was examined under five headings:

1. There is in Christ a nature superior to the human.
2. That this superior nature is pre-existent to the human.
3. That this pre-existent nature is divine.
4. That this divine nature is the deity of the Son of God.
5. That as the Son of God he is co-equal with the Father.

This typical evangelical approach began not with God's love, but with man's need. There were few references to contemporary theologians. Indeed, the only people quoted in the Lectures are the Scottish theologian, Thomas Chalmers, and the former Principal of Homerton College, Dr Pye-Smith.

Three important classes were held to enhance preaching gifts. A well-supported Monday evening Bible class was attended by many students and members of the church to discuss a given topic. On Thursday mornings one of the students read a prepared sermon which was then helpfully criticised by other students. Later that morning the whole student body discussed a given topic or passage of Scripture. Extempore contributions were encouraged, student confidence was increased, and light was shed on difficult subjects through this exercise. Up to 1888 'it has been doing good service in training in debate and in ready impromptu speech.'[53]

A record exists preserving the main features of the discussion class between 1868 and 1871. Subjects were proposed in the formal manner of a debating society and both staff and students were free to participate under the chairmanship of the Principal. Topics chosen embraced theological, devotional, ministerial and social issues. For instance, Hall proposed that 'Man was capable of promoting his own salvation'; Blandford debated whether the 'Saints will be judged with the wicked in the day of judgement' and it was abstrusely asked; 'Is there any communication of thought or feeling between embodied and disembodied spirits?' Unanswered prayer, unfulfilled prophecy, 'The propriety of using imposition of hands in setting apart church officers', the observing of the Lord's Supper, and the meaning of a scriptural call to ministry all claimed attention. Manning debated 'The influence of climate and scenery upon the mental and moral character of men', and the students' minds ranged over education, missionary work, total abstinence and the letting of property. Touches of humour appear in such popular student subjects as 'The manner in which students may turn their studies to the best account', 'The advantageous combination of preaching with study', and most explicitly, 'No examinations promote the main purpose of the College'. In 1870 they debated the relevant theme 'What may be the probable result of the Council now being held in Rome?' and the topic relevant for them every week 'Can ministers travel on Sundays consistently with their profession?'

It seems that on most subjects up to ten students would speak and then members of staff would have the concluding word. The topic 'the Peccability of Christ's Human Nature' lasted more than one class and produced seven student views and a divided faculty! Mr Gracey and Mr Fergusson were against the possibility of Christ sinning, Mr Rogers was in favour, since it made Christ 'a real man.'[54]

The high point of the week for most students was the lecture by the President on a Friday afternoon. He felt that preachers of the so-called 'simple gospel' should have a breadth of knowledge which would help to make their sermons clear, interesting and articulate. They should also be introduced to elementary techniques of public speaking. His lectures to his students were full of practicalities. He dealt with the use of the voice, its projection and modulation, the importance of posture to avoid the impression of slovenliness and the control of gestures. But his chief concern was not with the mechanics of sermon production and presentation, but with the preacher's spirituality.

In the series of published lectures, all given before 1879, he mainly deals with the minister's private life, preaching and illustrations. The first book of thirteen lectures pictures the pastor in the study guarding his own spiritual life, fulfilling his ministry of intercession, choosing the text, caring for his health. It contains special advice for those 'with slender apparatus' as pastors. The second book contains ten lectures stressing the importance in preaching of truth, the Holy Spirit and conversion. Proactical detail is given on open-air preaching, positive gesture and earnest manner. The third series contains eight lectures and two appendices, all on the gathering and use of illustrations and anecdotes. Books are recommended, literature and science explored, all with a view to illuminating the preached word.

Edgar R. Pullen, a student at the College in 1886–7, preserved contemporary notes of a year of Spurgeon's lectures. Thirty-three subjects are covered, dealing with practical and biblical topics. Familiar territory such as 'errors in speaking', 'preparation of a sermon', 'preaching from experience', 'soul-winning', 'anecdotes', and 'open-air preaching', is expanded to include biographical material on Ambrose, Augustine and Bernard, historial material on the Baptists, devotional topics such as 'religious doubt' and 'the promises of God', and doctrinal topics such as 'inspiration'. There are ten biblical lectures all aimed at illustrating the art of preaching. These embrace Genesis, prophecy, John the Baptist, Luke's Gospel, the journeys of Paul, Colossians, and the Pastoral Epistles. The content is practical and the style ordered. Most lectures have enumerated headings[55] and one example shows how a passage of Scripture was commented upon as it was read. This practice was common in Baptist worship and twenty-six comments are recorded in an 'expositional reading' of Luke 1.

Students were assessed by half-yearly examinations. No actual examination results exist, but an Assessment Book covers the years of the 1880 decade.[56] In it each tutor makes a comment upon the general performance of each man. Of 180 students recorded; forty-six were to serve overseas, so the vision of the men was wide. Of the thirty-one who began their course in 1885, only seven had mental abilities above average. Phrases occur such as 'education defective', 'he has never reached the advanced classes', 'an average man', 'slow in development', 'I fancy he will do!' James Spurgeon was scathing in some of his comments—'bad temper', 'does no work', 'I do not believe in him', 'weak', 'not much as a student', 'plodding'. Comments mainly concern preaching gift and character development. Of students listed between January 1882 and September 1889, only eighteen failed to complete their course, mainly due to ill health or domestic circumstances.

Apart from preparation for Classics and Mathematics classes, little demand was made on a student's personal time. This was left free for preaching and pastoral opportunities. All lectures were delivered in popular illustrative form and allowed adequate time for discussion so that students might learn to express their ideas. The large, well-selected library was provided to enrich their grasp of language. Their developing gifts were exercised as they went out to preach in the open air, in hired halls, stables and garages. *The Daily Telegraph* of 9 May 1879 gave a popular impression of the students' impact: 'Suddenly a change sprang up, numbers of young men... went out... preaching a crusade against indifference... they were warmly received by the people to whom they appealed.' J.C. Carlile claimed more ambitiously that their influence changed the current of religious teaching in England.[57] In an obituary of Spurgeon, George Lorimer wrote: 'The curriculum of the Pastors' College was devised and inaugurated as an institution for practical equipment and as such it has unquestionably justified its existence.'[58]

Archibald Fergusson spoke in 1890 of house-to-house visitation undertaken by students in the most destitute localities in the south of London as 'an education not to be found in books and classrooms. Only in immediate contact with human nature soaked with suffering can we really learn our work.'[59] This work was organised into the College Home Visiting Society with Mr Rumsey as Secretary. The students visited in pairs, handing out printed sermons to each household in the district. Consequently they 'will all manage personal conversations with readiness.'[60]

Several decayed, weak or young churches were adopted by the students. Through their preaching and visitation these grew strong enough to support their own pastor. David Gracey commented: 'Very rich has been the blessing outpoured upon the work done at some of these advanced posts.'[61] An example was Gipsy Road Baptist Church, West Norwood, with the Rev. Walter Hobbs as its pastor. His training at the College evoked 'profound gratitude and high appreciation'.[62] It had developed his natural gifts, quikened his spiritual impulses and strengthened his faith in God. At the beginning of his course in 1875 he was sent to preach at a large mission room in Norwood New Town, erected at personal cost by Mr E.J. Everett, a former Plymouth Brother. The eleven people present 'appreciated the ministry',[63] and asked him to return each succeeding month until, after three years, they issued a formal call to the pastorate and enlarged the building at a cost of £1,000. By 1882 the membership numbered 180. Spurgeon took the warmest interest in the project so near to his own residence and became its Treasurer and liberal benefactor. He also maintained a warm personal contact with the pastor: 'His oversight... was watchful and sympathetic and clearly he had high confidence in him.'

Evening Classes

In 1887 Spurgeon's College had 110 students, which enabled 'careful and judicious' selection.[63] Many of them came through the evening classes which 'had been a great source of supply to the college' and also a means of 'sending out colporteurs, city missionaries, lay preachers, Sabbath-school teachers and workers of all sorts.' This aspect of the work, known as 'The Christian Working Men's College', offered free education to anyone preparing for Christian service. By 1877 there were between two and three hundred names on the books. There was a fine spirit and efficient teaching.

Evening classes had been pioneered by King's College in London in 1849. Eighty-three students had attended some or all of the experimental classes provided for employed men. These classes were revived in 1855, soon after F.D. Maurice had established another series of evening lectures in London in connection with his Working Men's College. Eventually King's College provided a means of ministerial training through evening lectures, in a bid to boost flagging numbers. Most theological colleges in the mid-nineteenth century found it necessary to provide some elementary instruction for ill-educated students.

Spurgeon's classes helped the inadequate beginner with his education and made the benefits of the College's classes available to a wider clientele. The classes began in 1862 in the same rooms at the Tabernacle used by the College, to help any young man over sixteen prepare for effective Christian service. Some came from non-Baptist churches, some were unable to read or write, but all were tutored according to ability.

By 1867 the curriculum included the Classics, Mathematics, Natural Science, and other branches of liberal education. They operated in the following way:

Monday	8.30 p.m.	Bible Class	Mr Rogers
		Writing Class	Mr C.D. Evans
Tuesday	7.30 p.m.	Elementary English	Mr C.D. Evans
Wednesday	7.30 p.m.	Advanced English	Mr A. Fergusson
		Elementary Greek & Latin	Mr W. Durban
		Advanced Greek & Latin	Mr D. Gracey
	8.00 p.m.	French	Mr W. Durban
		Science	Mr W.R. Selway[64]

Mr Fergusson's English class included a monthly debate on appointed subjects, where two students read short papers giving opposite viewpoints which were then discussed, to encourage clear thinking and concise expression. These papers were gathered up into a manuscript magazine produced by the students.

Mr Evans' English class totalled about forty each week; others were enrolled but could only attend spasmodically due to pressure of business. A few came to the Monday writing class. More used Dr Morrell's *Parsing and Composition* to study elocution and analysis on Tuesday.[65] Advanced English included the reading aloud of prepared essays so that potential preachers could practise diction.

Linguistic and scientific studies for evening-class students ran parallel to those used with the full-time day students. John Jackson, a pastor at Sevenoaks, spoke of the pleasure and advantages he received through the classes:

> 'Here the mental culture of young men in business may be added. Such as are anxious to work for the Lord... may derive extraordinary assistance. This was my own experience. For two years I was thus helped in my business and at the same time in my Christian life and work. On entering College I found nothing new. I was acquainted with the tutors and the students and to some extent with all the subjects for study. The Evening Classes afforded the best preparation for the College and for the ministry. Poverty is no disqualification. Here is the way for all who have the will.'[66]

The evening-class route was taken by many young men. In the mid-1860s the number registered exceeded 150; in 1873 the number attending each week was seventy, about one-third of those registered.[67] In 1887 the students travelled from places like King's Cross, Hackney, Burdett Road, New Cross, Denmark Hill and Wandsworth.[68] That year the greatest interest was in the class studying Hodge's *Outlines of Theology*. The Greek class had read John's Gospel and there had been times of corporate prayer and praise.

In 1888 Spurgeon hinted that 'this part of our work does not command such numbers of men as it used to do',[69] for Board Schools and Polytechnics now supplied much of the elementary education and there were more distracting amusements to keep young men from study.[70] Many young men had however passed from the classes into the College, saving tutors the drudgery of elementary teaching: others had secured enhanced business prospects through the education received in the evening classes, with their increasing diversity of curriculum: Elizabethan History and Literature and 'Grecian' History were now included in the weekly programme in order to take students beyond the elementary education of the Board Schools.

The essence of the programme was flexibility. For some students the course was shortened. More able students could be sent to other colleges for further study.[71] In a similar way Spurgeon could say of the evening classes, 'Our endeavour is to adapt to each man's capacity... we have no stereotyped rules and are bound to nothing.'[72] As in other ventures, the President took a lead. He pioneered a Friday night popular lecture for men, charging twopence for admission. Subjects were mainly of an historical or biographical kind and pioneered the course that the evening classes took.

Material Resources

As the work of the College grew in reputation, applications were received from all parts of the United Kingdom, Germany, Portugal, Italy, British America and the United States. Such expansion made great demands on buildings and financial outlay. From 1861–73 the College was conducted in the rooms under the Metropolitan Tabernacle. During this time numbers rose from fifteen to nearly 150 and larger buildings erected in the immediate neighbourhood robbed the college rooms of natural light. Gas lamps were often burnt all day and all artificial lighting in this period consumed oxygen heavily, so lectures were conducted in increasingly stifling conditions. This affected student concentration and general health.

The Sword and the Trowel of 1873 displayed the front view of a design for two-storey 'New Buildings for the Pastors' College' on land purchased at the rear of the Tabernacle.[73] The design, in red brick with stone dressings, by Mr Currey of Norfolk Street, Strand, managed to cover every available inch of an odd-shaped piece of land. The ground floor would consist of a large hall suitable for conference gatherings, with movable partitions to form classrooms to be used on Sundays and weekdays. On the first floor the main college lecture room and library would be situated, with roof lighting by lantern to give maximum ground space. J.C. Carlile recalled the plan from personal memory:

> On the ground floor a large hall, a students' common room, the arena in which student gladiators fought, mixing metaphors and chopping logic. The assembly hall was on the first floor; there conferences were held upon which occasions the clans gathered from the ends of the earth and the chief of the clan sat at the middle table.... On the same floor there were small classrooms and the famous room at the end of the corridor where trial sermons were preached and many tears shed.

The foundation stone was laid on 14 October 1873 and the building opened eleven months later. The total cost of £15,000 was met by 1876: £3,000 was given in memory of a husband, £2,000 was a legacy from a reader of Spurgeon's sermons, £1,000 was raised by the generosity of former students, and other gifts came from interested churches and Tabernacle members. Two years later a trust fund was operative in which sufficient money was set aside to pay for repairs and rates, once the freehold had been purchased from the Ecclesiastical Commissioners.

The permanent trust deed was executed in January 1877. The property was vested in the trusteeship of the pastors of the Tabernacle and eleven deacons. All accounts were examined by church auditors and passed by the church meeting. The financial backing of the church was something upon which Spurgeon relied heavily. In a letter to the members of 6 November 1886, he thanks them for helping 'in my life work of the College for these many years'. He indicates that he has never liked to press the weekly offerings for the College—it has been an act of love for him and his chosen work; yet £36 5s is required for each week and this has not been reached recently. Therefore, 'I shall take it as proof of your esteem and confidence if you will make this up by two collections on November 14.... Please come next Lord's day with such an offering as you judge that the College demands.'[74]

A small finance committee, the pastors and two deacons, managed the affairs of the College, and monthly figures of income and expenditure were published from the mid-sixties. In December 1865 the total income was £201 16s 1d; by July 1867 it had risen to £495 per month. The 1865 accounts show such named donors as 'Mr Dodwell', 'Mrs Baker', 'Amy'; anonymous gifts from 'A Christian brother', 'R.W.', 'Faith and a Friend'; church gifts from 'Chelsea', 'Woolwich', 'Wandsworth', and 'Southampton' and weekly offerings from the Tabernacle totalling £108.[75] In the 1867 account there is 'a birthday gift for Mr Spurgeon' of £33, four collections from churches where Spurgeon had preached and a thank-offering for him of £73.[76]

By 1877 Spurgeon believed that college finances were on a firm footing. No great increase in funds would be required and income came from three main sources—Tabernacle offerings totalling £1,880, donations amounting to £3,153, and student collections of just over £400. Barod and lodging accounted for over half the expenditure, salaries for one fifth. The work of preaching stations and College Conference claimed one seventh, whilst books took only £350 out of total payments of £7,489. In that year there was a surplus of £1,500. In the following year 'from an accountant's point of view the ordinary income is at least £1,000 below the exenditure,' but 'usually a large legacy falls in just when the exchequer runs low.'[77] By now a growing number of students were able to bear their own costs, but no charges were ever published. About one tenth of the donations came from churches, all the rest from supporting individuals.

Spurgeon was never afraid to appeal for money, direct deacons of churches to cover students' expenses, or ask for a preaching fee which would be donated to the College. Yet he was unfailing in expressing thanks for the fact that the College never ran into debt, nor was its work curtailed for financial reasons. He realised that it was easier to raise money for the orphanage: 'Many will give to an orphanage out of natural compassion who will not contribute to a college out of zeal for the truth.'[78]

Supportive Agencies

The College recognised that 'Our ministers generally cannot afford to buy books and our desire is in some measure to supply this grievous want. A minister without a book is like a workman without tools.'[79] The College course had to be extensive in order to overcome ignorance and a circulating library was in operation from 1867 to help former students continue study after college. Boxes of books were sent in circuit to those settled as pastors in different parts of the country. These were kept for two months and then forwarded to the next in circuit. Thirty-four boxes were in circulation, containing Puritan literature, Spurgeon's books and advice about ministerial reading matter. Alternatively, deacons were asked to purchase books for a church library to which the pastor had access.

To check on the progress of former students the College Conference was formed in 1865. It met in March in successive years for five days, in 1867 changing to September. Ministers were scattered all over the country, some working in areas where there was no fellowship, some in villages where progress was slow, some in urban areas where circumstances were uncongenial to health and faith. It was soon recognised that a gathering was needed to encourage flagging spirits. The Conference constitution consisted of agreement about the doctrines of grace, believer's baptism and evangelism. The London Pastors were formed into a standing committee to deal with administration, organisation and discipline. Most administration was carried out by J.A. Spurgeon, the secretary. Membership was open to all students of six-months' standing or ministers who received three-quarters of the members' votes. Meetings were mostly held at the Tabernacle, but other venues such as Upton Chapel, Sloane Street Chapel and Stepney Green were used. On the Tuesday evening of Conference a dinner was usually held to invite present and past students to meet supporters and on these occasions it was not uncommon for £1,000 to be contributed to college funds.

During the first two conferences a great variety of papers were read and discussed. These included theological topics on the inspiration, study and exposition of Scripture; denominational topics such as the need for evangelists, the belief in the doctrines of grace, and the stance to be adopted towards the Established Church; ecclesiastical subjects such as eldership, duties of pastors, discipline and salaries; educational discussion on the best way of securing an educated ministry; pastoral themes on personal holiness, oneness of aim in the ministry, the conduct of prayer meetings and the use of printing; and evangelistic subjects such as the conversion of the young and the poor, and the temperance of ministers.

The happiness of such gatherings was marred by the Downgrade Controversy of 1888. This arose out of a series of articles in *The Sword and the Trowel*, the mouthpiece of Spurgeon's church (the Metropolitan Tabernacle), in the spring of 1887, and affected the whole Baptist family. The articles regretted and warned against the decline of Calvinism and the embracing by late nineteenth-century Christians of rationalistic theology and the assumptions of biblical criticism. They constituted a spiritual health-warning for the church, and contained allusions to unamed Baptist ministers who remained within the fellowship of the Baptist Union whilst clearly embracing those views which Spurgeon criticised. Reactions to the articles led to Spurgeon's resignation from the Baptist Union, and to subsequent attempts in the Council and Assembly to effect a reconciliation and reassure the denomination.

Press response and articles on the affair abound, yet coherent accounts are few.[80] Although the setting and chronology of the crisis are clear, the issues and personalities are bewildering. They continue to be more fully explored.[81]

At Spurgeon's College the Conference of old students was broken up and a new one formed. Membership now demanded adherence to a rigorous creed,[82] but in that creed it was specifically stated that adherents were not binding themselves to the teaching of Calvin or any other inspired man, nor was exact agreement necessary upon all disputed points of any system. What was vital was that:

> 'We utterly abhor the idea of a new gospel or an additional revelation or a shifting rule of faith to be adapted to the ever-changing spirit of the age. In particular we assert that the notion of probation after death and the ultimate restitution of condemned spirits is so unscriptural and unprotestant, so unknown to all Baptist confessions of faith and draws with it such consequences, that we are bound to condemn it, to regard it as one with which we can hold no fellowship.'[83]

The new Conference met on April 1888 as the 'Pastors' College Evangelical Association'. Members had to sign a doctrinal statement which contained evangelical sentiments. A committee was set up to enquire into cases of moral delinquency and a bye-law was incorporated, defining subject matter as that 'only for spiritual profit and for the promotion of the cause and kingdom of our Lord Jesus Christ.'[84] At the re-formed Conference 'the assembly of brethren was a larger one than on any former occasion.' The roll of membership stood at 546 with about another 100 expected to be added when they returned their signed doctrinal statement. This figure was less than half the total number of former students. But at the Tuesday evening dinner £3,700 was subscribed for the College, 50% more than ever before. This first re-formed Conference was a demonstration of support for Spurgeon, who was elected President for life. Concern for the brethren was also expressed in offerings for the Communion and Assurance Funds. The main papers at this Conference were on biblical reforms, such as Hezekiah's reform, and lessons for today from Philemon. Letters giving details of the Conference events were sent by the President and Secretary to all brethren abroad.

Contemporary students of the College during the controversy generally followed Spurgeon. There is no recorded reflection by Spurgeon on the effect of the controversy on students. One of the tutors, Archibald Fergusson, commented, in a full but partisan way, on the effects of the Downgrade Controversy on the religious life of the thoughtful student. He listed five effects:

1. An intensified desire for efficiency in preaching the old gospel.
2. A seeking of an increased assurance and certainty in preaching the gospel.
3. An intenser spirit of consecration to the person of the Lord Jesus.
4. An increased conviction that, unaided by the methods of the new theology, the gospel is in every way adequate to cope with and cure all the ills of the souls of fallen men.
5. A complete reliance on the Holy Spirit for true success. The language of the article is strong: 'The students are in loathing and disgust, they turn their backs on the flippant invention and subject almost every syllable of the sacred text and contexts, wherein these reviled truths are set forth, to a

Fig. 2.4 A typical group of late nineteenth century students.

crucial criticism.' F.G. Marchant, his colleague, concluded emphatically: 'I do not know of a single student who has shown any sympathy at any time with what is regarded as the new theology.'

A few former students resigned from the Baptist Union with Spurgeon. A significant number refused to conform to the new Conference expression of the doctrines of grace. Some probably needed the fellowship of the Union, some failed to comprehend Spurgeon's strategy; many respected their mentor but felt that he was behind the times, looking backward rather than forward. It is true that a hundred met to attempt a strategy of reconciliation, but even among his own supporters he did not receive the help that he anticipated. For instance, William Cuff of Shoreditch, a former Spurgeon's College graduate and pastor of the largest baptist church in London, questioned Spurgeon's approach. The attack on unnamed Baptist ministers as heretical meant that many fell under suspicion. Debate still rages over whom Spurgeon was referring to, but the ordinary pastor, like Cuff, must have felt that Spurgeon was attacking ministerial colleagues, who differed from him but whose friendship and fellowship Cuff and others valued. Cuff had the warmest relations with Thomas Tymms, his near neighbour at Down's Chapel, Clapton, of whom it was said that he 'shares in the larger hope'.[85] concerning the ultimate triumph of God's love. Cuff would have no desire to see men like Tymms excluded from the Baptist Union. Whatever the cause of his disagreement with Spurgeon, Cuff was not afraid 'to look him in the face and honestly say so', and to make it clear publicly that he had disagreed with Spurgeon over his methods.

Cuff was 'anxious to save the Union from a terrible disaster'.[86] More closely involved in the workings of the Union than Spurgeon had ever been, he needed the financial support of the richer churches for his work at Shoreditch Tabernacle. It would also seem he had information that the Downgrade Controversy was already causing concern and division among rural churches. Cuff had a special concern for such churches, having begun his preaching in them and because his first church was a rural cause. A further schism would cause even greater scandal and weaken the Baptist witness in the shires. Cuff hoped that Spurgeon would accept Dr Angus' evangelical declaration, even as amended by Dr Clifford. Certainly John Clifford believed that Rev. J.

Spurgeon and Mr Cuff would do their best to persuade Mr Spurgeon to accept modifications in the declaration.[87] Cuff probably even hoped to persuade Spurgeon to re-enter the Baptist Union.

Downgrade was not the first occasion when Spurgeon disagreed in public with other evangelicals. During the first ten years of his ministry in London, he had involved himself in two theological controversies within the Congregational denomination, entered into animated debate with the Baptist Missionary Society over fiscal policy, and lost nearly all his income from the sale of printed sermons in the United States because of his outspoken pronouncements on slavery. In 1864 he upset many evangelical Anglicans by a forthright sermon about baptismal regeneration, and as a result he resigned from the Evangelical Alliance. At the same time he shared in founding the London Baptist Association. Ironically, in 1888 he resigned from the London Baptist Association but received enthusiastic support from the Evangelical Alliance and members of the established church! Literary evidence in Spurgeon's College archives indicates that for four years between 1883 and 1887 he received numerous letters indicating disquiet over the doctrines being preached from many pulpits. He was urged to act. Yet when he did so over the central themes of Inspiration, Atonement and Eternal Punishment, he found that the number of those who supported him dwindled; and from being the accuser he became the accused.

He entered this controversy, as he had done all the others, in print; but this was of a new kind. It involved a growing and unified denomination, and he made obvious mistakes. He declined to name suspect ministers. He lessened the circle of influence around him. He declined to speak directly to the Assembly. He withdrew from the Union at too early a stage in the controversy. He refused to discuss the issues involved when the Baptist leaders sought to meet with him. He became an oasis surrounded by the Coleridgian affirmation of culture, the Darwinian commitment to evolution, the Maurician restatement of hell, the Congregational departure from biblical inerrancy, and a commitment of some Baptist ministers to restate Christian doctrine in contemporary terms.

He found his solution in independence. This had three effects. First, it led to the diminishing influence of Spurgeon in the latter years of his life. Second, it meant that his effective influence beyond his death was to be in those churches that adopted his own independent approach to fellowship. His influence in the Baptist Union, where fellowship is on a wider basis, bacame markedly more limited. Third, the effect on the College lasted until he died, but in the years after his death major changes took place as the College came to terms with late nineteenth-century life. Nevertheless, the institution continued to train Calvinistically-inclined pastor-evangelists, whose educational background was generally more slender and denominational commitment weaker than those of ministers from Regent's Park College. While Regent's also contributed to fashioning a concept of ministry among Baptists that was linked with office in the wider Christian Church, Spurgeon's concept was narrower, defined as function within the local church. The division caused by Downgrade had important ministerial, denominational and ecumenical implications.

To avoid flooding the ministerial market many of the

students went to establish new work rather than to invade existing churches. The breadth of this work was the world. By 1863 thirty-eight men had gone into churches, including one to Australia, one to Ireland, two to Wales and one to a Primitive Methodist Circuit. J. Turner ventured to Newfoundland, T.W. Hayward went to Lancashire, eleven settled in London churches and a similar number went into East Anglia.[88] By 1873, 330 men had been trained at the College, of whom two were in India, one in China, two in Spain, one in Brazil, one in St Helena, one in Turk's Island, one in South Africa, six in Australia, twenty-three in the United States and ten in Canada. On 2 November 1880 eight brethren serving in Australia sent a letter to Spurgeon expressing gratitude for their course of training:

> 'No words of ours can express our personal obligation to you. But by fidelity to Christ and to truth, by manifesting that we have caught the spirit of burning love to souls which burns in your own breast, and by serving to our utmost ability, we hope to show that all your care and that of the tutors and friends of the Tabernacle has not been ill-bestowed.'[89]

The main outreach was however in London. In 1864 a loan fund was established administered by deacons of the Tabernacle to enable churches to build anew or reduce debts. Loans were repayable half-yearly. The expiicit objectives were 'To assist by gift or loan, without interest, in the building, enlargement and repair of places used for divine worship and... the furtherance of any object having regard to maintenance of the Pastors' College.'[90] At a meeting in the Tabernacle on 10 November 1865 the London Baptist Association was formed, with these agreed aims: 'To advance the Kingdom of Christ... the promotion of Christian union amongst the officers and members, and the erection of at least one chapel in each year in the the Metropolis or its suburbs.'[91]

In his detailed study of London Baptist life, W.T. Whitley states that 'the number of churches founded between 1860–70 and the number surviving has never been equalised before or since.' Yet, he continues, 'While they were busy as beavers they were as unsociable as otters; they multiplied at an unprecedented rate but each was isolated at first.'[92] In 1841, 102 Baptist churches functioned in London. By 1900, 102 new churches had been added, largely founded by men from Pastors' College. In this striking growth Spurgeon acted as a lynch-pin—people looked to him for leadership and he gave adventurous expression to his evangelistic zeal. He had founded a college 'to train men who would be able to present the gospel in the language of the common people' and the institution 'set out upon a mission of its own'.[93]

A series of contemporary letters now in the College archives, illustrates Spurgeon's superintendency of affairs.[108] F.W. Reynolds reflects that so many deacons 'were seeing you just now...'. S.C. Gordon desires to go with the Baptist Missionary Society to Congo 'with your consent'. C.H. Hands is returning to America and asks candidly, 'What would you advise me to do?' J.C. Carlile wants to know whether he can stay at Abbey Street, Bermondsey, in spite of financial hardships: 'If you could kindly spare me five minutes I think the matter might be settled.' Spurgeon wanted Mr Loma to go to Tangier, but Providence Baptist Chapel, Hounslow, desired him as their pastor. It took pleas by the retiring minister, church secretary, and a petition signed by fifty-four members to gain the President's consent. Trinity Baptist Church, Bexleyheath, expressed their indebtedness to Spurgeon by placing a copy of *The Sword and the Trowel* beneath the foundation stone of their new chapel in 1868. One of their early pastors, the Rev. William Frith, was converted at the Tabernacle. in 1870 one of their members, Mr Spoffard, was commended for training at the Pastors' College and in 1873, when Mr Frith resigned, 'a small deputation waited upon the Rev. C.H. Spurgeon to seek his advice.'[94]

R.H. Gillespie, the student who began the church at Plaistow, recorded the beginning of the venture in a letter to Spurgeon:

> 'On February 23rd 1872 you sent for me to come and see you in your vestry. On going there I found you had company, four gentlemen whom I had never seen before. You then addressed me thus: "Gillespie, I want you to go down to Barking Road and preach for two or three Sundays and if you don't like the place don't stay; if you do, stick to it. I'll help to support you. These gentlemen have come for you".'[95]

Such marching orders were common. Not only were men dismissed to new work, they went to revive old causes. Nor were they sent only into the suburbs of London. Many declining provincial churches were aided in places such as Tonbridge, in Kent; Ryde, on the Isle of Wight; South Shields and Middlesborough on Teeside; Harston in rural Cambridgeshire and Whitehaven in Cumberland. Most students faced an uphill task in their initial pastorates.

In 1879 Spurgeon divulged his pioneering strategy:

> 'The plan is generally to begin in a hall or other hired building, to get together a few people, to gather converts and to struggle on

till a small church is formed; then commence the labour of collecting money to build a school-room or part of a building or to erect an iron chapel, and this accomplished the chapel is undertaken. Thus by degrees with slender funds a new house of prayer is opened and Christian activities set in motion.'[96]

He admitted that many such experiments failed to produce churches and felt the provision of a settled building was the key to success. In 1859 the Assembly Rooms of the Spread Eagle Tavern in Wandsworth were hired and, after J.W. Genders had preached for three months, a small church was formed of nine members under his pastoral oversight. By 1863 the membership numbered 150 and a £3,000 chapel was opened to become East Hill Baptist Church. In Stepney the East London Tabernacle began in the hall of the Beaumont Institute in 1858. It had a building by 1864, enlarged by 1869, at a cost of £12,000. The generosity of the Christian builder, gifts from the College and the proceeds of the sale of a nearby Methodist Chapel met the expenditure. South Street, Greenwich, took twenty years of 'patient and unwearied toil'[97] before a church could be erected and the members move out of the Royal Hill Lecture Hall. Initial work in Bromley with open-air preaching in the market place and meetings in the White Hart Assembly Rooms declined to six people in 1862, but by 1863 a church of thirty members was formed in a house and by 1865 a building had been erected. A church in Upper Kennington Lane began in a carpenter's shop and then took over St Paul's Anglican Church. The pastor, Mr G. Hearson, then took a course at the College. The church in Lewin Road, Streatham, began as a preaching station in mobile accommodation. Barnes Baptist Church was erected by a wealthy gentleman who in 1868 called a student, W.H. Priter, to gather a congregation. Enfield Baptist Church started in the Rising Sun Public House.

In 1883 George Rogers commented on the evangelistic tone of the College: 'Our one chief desire is to be distinguished for our zeal for the spiritual and eternal welfare of our fellow men.'[98]

Spurgeon recalled how his own fervour and gift began to be enriched through involvement in education when he started addressing Sunday school in a regular fashion: 'Speedily something else followed. The older people also took to coming when I spoke; and that, 'ere long, in such numbers that the auditory look more like a chapel than a school.'[99] He recognised the link between evangelism and education and Spurgeon's College attempted through an appropriate educational environment and curriculum to train evangelistic church planters.

CHAPTER 3

The Tabernacle
1892–1922

WHEN CHARLES HADDON SPURGEON, the founder of the Pastors' College, died at the untimely age of fifty-seven his church, and those institutions associated with it, were plunged into a crisis of leadership. In *The Sword and the Trowel,* A.T. Pierson, the temporary preacher at the Tabernacle after Spurgeon's death, indicated the four unchanging characteristics of the Pastor's College. He highlighted the College's commitment to the authority and plenary inspiration of the Word of God, and the desire to express in a definite form of words the treasure of faith contained within the Scriptures. Second, he meant a continuing commitment to Calvinistic theology and its doctrines of predestination, substitutionary atonement and everlasting punishment. Third the College was committed to the right balance of intellectual expertise and spiritual character. Finally the College was to take students who were committed full-time to the preaching of the gospel and were therefore able to undertake study and Christian work unhindered and unfettered by the constraints of secular employment.

Throughout the thirty years after Spurgeon's death, repeated affirmations were made that the College was continuing the Calvinistic and fundamental theological position which Spurgeon had insisted should be taught dogmatically by the tutors:[1] 'Whatever other institutions may do it is the firm determination of the Pastors' College to stand by the old flag held so nobly and tenaciously to the last by its beloved founder';[2] 'The doctrines that were, still continue to be those things which are most surely believed among us';[3] 'Our helpers may rest quite satisfied that no new theology will be taught. We are all wedded to the old.' In this 1908-9 edition of *The Sword and the Trowel* there was an urgent appeal for funds, no mention of Tabernacle gifts,[4] and continuing commitment that candidates should have been preaching for at least two years and have shown proven effectiveness and fruitfulness in Christian service. Yet during this thirty-year period the College moved from a situation where Spurgeon as 'the Governor' dominated the whole enterprise, through a transitional period where 'the leaders' of the Tabernacle Church and Spurgeon's twin sons, Charles and Thomas, had oversight of the work, to a position where an emerging College Council contained widespread representation far beyond the resources of the Tabernacle. No longer was the leadership of Council and the College to be in the hands of those called Spurgeon, although the name of the institution itself was changed from Pastors' to Spurgeon's College. Further the College moved from the building at the rear of the Tabernacle in Newington Butts to its present site at the Falkland Park Estate.

Evaluation

Throughout the metamorphosis the hallmarks of C.H. Spurgeon survived. There was the emphasis on prayer, faith, the gospel, Scripture and the Holy Spirit. Prayer was paramount. It was the channel of spiritual resources. Spurgeon was a man of prayer who found a hidden source of strength which never failed him in time of need. It was the spirit and practice of prayer which brought revival to the waning New Park Street Chapel. The prayers of his people remained throughout his ministry a source of strength and encouragement.

A firm faith in the sovereignty and love of God sustained Spurgeon at the beginning of his ministry in London when he was slandered, criticised and lampooned. Faith held him when aspersions were cast on his character, when the reality of his conversion was doubted, and when his motives were questioned. Towards the end of his ministry when the clouds of controversy darkened the sky, his faith did not waver.

In the gospel he found inexhaustible resources. He saw God at work as people were brought to Christ wherever he preached. He was steeped in the Scriptures. His biblical addresses showed a man whose own thirst was quenched day by day at this source of living water.

In all these resources the Spirit of God was at work. Charles Haddon Spurgeon depended for his success upon the influence of the Spirit and the prayers of his people. Not immune to criticism, he came under attack because strict Cavinists saw him as a liberal Arminian, whereas others felt that he preached a hard reactionary gospel. Traditional churchmen, even of his own denomination, were often appalled by his pulpit presentation: 'a vulgar ranter—an unlettered boy who dared to tell jokes in the pulpit and to pray as though he were on intimate terms with his Creator.'[5] Carlile however believed that Spurgeon was merely open to misinterpretation, because he spoke the language of the common people.[6]

Spurgeon was also criticised for his egotism, and certainly many of his sermons, lectures and literary works contained many references to self, his own experience, his own testimony and his own personality. His egotism was, however, balanced by his conviction that he was but an instrument, 'a frail tool, useful only because his Lord willed his success.'[7] Other criticism was levelled at him for his liberal life-style, his winter visits to the South of France, his wealth—'rumour said that Spurgeon would die a very wealthy man, but rumour was disappointed.'[8] His resignation from the denomination limited his influence. The institution also needed to adapt its work to changing circumstances.

The Emphasis in Ministry

The College needed to evaluate the type of minister being trained in the light of changing denominational expectations and sociological needs. Many Baptists regarded churches without a minister as 'destitute and distressed'.[9] The minister's role included teaching, watching over the flock, preaching, praying, visiting the sick, the tempted and the destressed when required, and abiding by the flock through good and ill. Only the pastor ordained to the oversight of a local church would normally administer baptism and the Lord's Supper.

The local church sought its own pastor, looking for a man with a gift for preaching, discreet conduct and exemplary life. The procedure would involve a corporate day of prayer and fasting, election of a vacancy committee, advice about the names of possible ministers, and consultation with other pastors and congregations. The nominee would normally undertake a period of probationary preaching at the vacant church and then receive a call to the pastorate. He would become a member of that church before being recognised as pastor.

Early Baptist ecclesiology had its roots in Separatist covenant theology; the importance of the local church as a group of gathered believers gave a very sharply-focused emphasis on ministry. The primary stress was on the priesthood of *all* believers, and out of that developed emphasis on the leadership of *some*. A pastor or presiding elder would be set apart from within the local congregation and his ministry was limited to that local congregation.

Although the General Baptist tradition had a wider view of the Church ealier than Particular Baptists did, by the beginning of the nineteenth century both groups had developed in their understanding beyond the merely local. This had happened partly because of the development of Association life under political pressure in the mid-seventeenth century, partly because of the influences of connectionalism in revivalist Methodism, and partly because of the very formation of structures like the General Baptist Assembly. Calvinistic Baptists also broadened their theology of fellowship and culture. Throughout the nineteenth century the doctrine of independency was tenaciously upheld, yet pragmatism recognised its deficiencies and the need to express concepts of ministry in wider terms.

Relationships within a local church ought to be cemented with love, service and submission, but practice did not always match the theory. A domineering minister, a strong-willed congregation, a young man presenting new theological ideas, a strongly conservative church, people who held the purse-strings or were ambitious for office—any of these could make the fellowship degenerate into sour confrontation. A tyrannical church could trample on the servant-pastor. Baptists were clear about the role and function of the pastor, refusing to entertain sacerdotal ideas or priestly functions, but recognising the need for training and professionalism, to secure the status of pastors in an increasingly mobile society. Baptists had to face up to the reality of a recognised ministry beyond the local church, and take account of connexionalism in terms of ministerial validation.

A major aim in forming the Baptist Union in 1812 was to make better provision for the training and maintenance of ministers. The Union envisaged one of its chief tasks as increasing the supply of godly and learned ministers. The Union Handbook for 1867 contained an alphabetical list of Baptist ministers with their places of ministry. The note at the top states: 'Great pains have been taken to make this list as accurate as possible. The Editor will be thankful to be informed of any errors or omissions so that they may be corrected or supplied in future issues.'[10] It was apparently sufficient for a minister to ask for his name to be inserted. From 1869 the college where the minister had been trained was inserted where relevant and the year in which he commenced his ministry. The list carries this note: 'Names are added to the list only on the recommendation of tutors of colleges, secretaries of Associations, three accredited Baptist ministers or three members of the Baptist Union Committee.' The 1889 Handbook went a stage further: 'A name is placed on this list by vote of the Council of the Baptist Union who require a recommendation from the tutors of colleges, by secretaries of Associations or by three members of the Council.' It is more than likely that the Trustees had funds to which the impecunious minister could apply for assistance, and found this list to be increasingly useful, as some kind of commendation. Once the Baptist Union wanted to augment stipends to make ministry possible for poor churches, central administration needed clear rules.

In 1896 the Assembly set up a Ministerial Recognition Committee, whose task it was to prevent the unworthy and unfit from entering the ministry, to assist those whom God had called and qualified for the pastorate by commending them to churches of the denomination, and to secure for such pastors, among other privileges, eligibility to benefit from the funds of the Union. The Union emphasised the need for collegiate training, and the colleges became catalysts for denominational centralisation, although arrangements were also made for non-collegiate candidates to sit an examination to qualify for the accredited list.

In the nineteenth century there were two conflicting influences. The first was a greater sense of professionalism among ministers, brought about by the Union and colleges, and by trends in society. People wanted a ministry that was distinct, full-time, and educated, in an age when society at large was increasingly educated and people were prepared to take a pragmatic approach to matters like ministry. In a denomination which had always stressed the role of elders and teachers in plurality of leadership within a local congregation, the ministry of one paid pastor as a Ruling Elder or leading minister was emerging. The movement of such ministers from one congregation to another within a more mobile society, influenced by the Methodist itinerancy, became a marked feature. On the other hand, the anti-Tractarian movement was wary of the title 'Reverend', denied the importance of ordination, and dismissed the practice of laying on of hands. Preaching was exalted as the major function of the minister and great stress was set on oratorical gifts in any assessment of ministerial capacity.

Within the dissenting tradition there was always a strong emphasis on the theocratic rule of Christ by his Spirit within the local congregation, and so the style of any leader needed to be inspirational, democratic or participatory. High value was placed on the evident spiritual gifts of the leader. This arose partly through Nonconformist ecclesiology and partly through a Calvinistic theology which viewed culture with suspicion and therefore saw Christ as the converter of culture. There was a narrow focus on the doctrine of redemption and the work of the Spirit in the life of the regenerate believer, with consequent neglect of the doctrine of creation and of an appreciation of natural and academic gifts.

Spurgeon's College was training pastor-evangelists for church planting. Such students had a keen pioneering spirit, but their commitment to denominational structures was tentative. The new century demanded better-educated pastors, able to edify the faithful with penetrating exposition of Scripture. The College needed to raise its educational standards to meet the new requirements.

The Nature of Theological Training

Part of the work of any theological college is to develop those qualities indispensable for ministry. Different people would set these qualities in a different order of priority. Some would look for assertiveness, ability to argue rationally, learning and scholarship, scriptural interpretation, individual ruggedness, and personal independence before God. Others would point to complementary qualities—passivity, quietness, intuition, feelings and emotional experiences, personal intimacy, interdependence, reflective spirituality, and a sense of community.

The predominant nineteenth-century model for ministerial training was the seminary model. Likely candidates for the ministry were institutionalised for a period of time during which they received teaching, to sharpen their minds and develop their gifts so that with skill, expertise and zeal they could fulfil the role to which they were called by God and set apart by the Church. Such a model allowed little scope for contextualisation, nor for experiential or reflective learning. It allowed little opportunity for students to discover theology in ways which grew directly out of their world, to discover how faith and the world around were inextricably linked. This lack lay behind some of the fears expressed about nineteenth-century institutional training.

Involvement in a full-time training course within a theological college community ensures that any misunderstanding of ministry, such as seeking status, authority and power, or envisaging some mystique about the minister or his work, can be corrected: ministry is no more and no less than service for Jesus Christ. Training within a community gives a person a renewed sense of solidarity with Christ and his Church and develops an understanding of the corporate reality of the Body of Christ. The student benefits from recognising the real theological diversity between Christians, which has to be met head-on. Students learn to appreciate others' points of view, with a degree of tolerance and humility about their own convictions. Such personal interaction develops self-knowledge. It is not only a matter of learning how to handle disagreements and confrontations, but also of discovering one's personal propensity for anger and vulnerability, of coming to terms with one's own inadequacies and of appreciating one's strengths. Pastoral care takes on a new dimension, as people become aware of their responsibility for others over the whole field of faith and experience. Students share responsibility for the worship of the community. Colleges are committed to the discipline of biblical, historical and theological study—ongoing priorities for pastors. Nineteenth-century students testify to the formative influence of fellow trainees within a residential community. Personality, doctrinal views, academic preferences and practical skills are all influenced even more by friends than tutors.

Theological college students learn not only by instruction but by induction: as well as being taught in the classroom, they learn from their environment about people and society and how the Church can relate to such people. Most of the London theological colleges[10] engaged their students in regular work among the poor and many of them were housed in private dwellings widely dispersed around the captial. Most London college students lived in north and west London, only Spurgeon's had large numbers located south of the river. After 1856 when Stepney College was relocated to Regent's Park there was no college in east London. This meant that few students were exposed to the poverty, powerlessness and helplessness that pervaded many working-class areas after the mid-Victorian era. They did not experience at first-hand what working people were going through and so failed to understand their antipathy towards religion. Colourful ritualist, ardent evangelical, and even the exuberant revivalist, would be proclaiming the gospel to people about whose lives they had little understanding. Spurgeon's College had the best opportunity, because of its location and the placement of its students amongst families, to get to grips with the realities of working-class life in Southwark. Even so, this opportunity was limited because Tabernacle families tended to be 'respectable' lower middle-class people and the students had little time over from their studies for taking stock of their social surroundings.

Students, taught to plant churches, were not taught how to perfect them and make them a creditable witness to the gospel among people who had a negative self-image, feeling deprived, lonely and unable to control their own destiny. Such people needed to be given hope and fresh vision by pastors who understood and sympathised with their plight. At Spurgeon's College every spare minute outside the classroom was given to practical Christian activity, in preaching, evangelistic and pastoral work.

Spurgeon's College was weak academically. It never instituted an entrance examination, yet attempted a classical curriculum. The frenetic activity was rarely evaluated. The spiritual life of students was better cultivated than at Regent's Park, although the academic life was weaker. Regent's men, graduating from London University, made a stronger contribution to Baptist thought. Spurgeon's men were independently busy, but rarely encouraged to participate in denominational structures. In all Nonconformist training there was inadequate emphasis on self-awareness and personal relationships—essential tools for effective ministry in connexional ecclesiology.

During a college course, Anglican ordinands were very limited in their practical opportunities because of restrictions placed upon them until ordination. Nonconformists had more freedom. Early in the century dissenting academics made a strategic contribution to itinerant evangelism. From 1850 onwards the activity of preaching societies was more devoted to establishing and developing new congregations. Church planting was an important goal of student industry. In college preaching exercises, worship and preaching were divorced, so that, in the newly planted congregations, preaching was the paramount act in a service and all else was viewed as preliminary. Sacraments were not celebrated in the Nonconformist colleges and this contributed to their continued debasement in dissenting worship. Although tutors read students' sermons, they rarely preached in front of the students. Without a good model for style and content, uniting classroom study with pulpit expression, students relied only on correction and practice to enhance their gifts. Before students entered the college, testimonials bore witness to the soundness of their doctrinal position. During the course opportunities to develop an open, flexible, independent and mature mind were limited. Up to 1880 this deficiency was not seriously exposed, thanks to the religious continuity of the century. In the next twenty years, when change was rapid, the dangers became more obvious. Admission procedures paid little attention to the depths of personality or the candidate's place in the world. The structure of college life encouraged the development of industrious, punctual, systematic, thorough and hard-working pastors, but the complementary qualities of sensitivity, reflectivity and interdependence were not fostered. The move to Falkland Park made it possible to develop a residential community for students.[11]

The Content of Training

The College needed to evaluate its educational philosophy. Averse to popery, Spurgeon's College yet evidenced much in common with approaches to learning among Roman Catholics, whose seminaries favoured verbatim note-taking and rote learning, on the assumption that the truths of revelation could be learned as a set of propositions, to be handed on and defended, but not explored by the ordinary cleric.

Exegesis of Scripture occupied an important place in some London colleges, but left limited scope for developing the subject. Even at Spurgeon's, where concern for ministry dominated the timetable, there was a commitment to study of the classics, for tradition died hard. All colleges lengthened courses in a quest for wider and deeper studies, but none saw the course as the beginning of a lifetime of study. In the Anglican colleges, episcopal oversight helped to keep the religious aspect to the fore; at Congregational New College and Baptist Regent's Park, the stimulus of London University encouraged scholarship, at Methodist Richmond College and at Spurgeon's, keen evangelistic zeal fashioned the framework of learning. Ideally spirituality, scholarship and evangelism should blend in evident balance, but no London college achieved this satisfactorily in the nineteenth-century.

The traditional Baptist fear of learning as a barrier to the working of the Spirit was constantly voiced and as frequently combatted. Regent's Park College set out to train pastor-teachers who would work within denominational structures at home or overseas and primarily address the needs of the church, perfecting saints and expounding the Word. Working closely with the university, Regent's concentrated particularly on biblical languages and exegesis. At Spurgeon's, where the role of pastor-evangelist and pioneering church planter was always dominant, such spiritual qualities as zeal, prayer and calling were mentioned more frequently than academic gifts or educational success. The Regent's pastor-teacher was equipped for a distinct role as leader of the congregation, representing the wider Church; the Spurgeon tradition represented an alternative Baptist view which emphasised the ministry of all and the anointed leadership of some, whose training was down-to-earth and practical. The major weakness of this approach lay in an unwillingness to embrace modern insights and a failure to stretch students to their maximum limits mentally, so that they in turn could build up thinking Christians. Again, Baptists neglected the corporate dimension of the Church and trained ministers likely to be individualistic and isolationist.

Spurgeon's College was committed to a practical curriculum designed to promote the preaching gift. The content was primarily the doctrine of the atonement, derived from an exposition of Scripture and aimed at the conversion of individuals. There was little interest in ecclesiology, worship or sacraments, nor in denominational or historical perspective. Baptists emphasised the Scriptures and the individual relationship with Christ. The corporate dimension of the church found little place within this brand of evangelicalism.

Classical study was intended to enhance the prospective minister's mind and shape his character, but Latin and Greek studies, demanding hard work and consuming many hours, included little of direct relevance to the students' understanding of the Scriptures. Such study would, however, help to sharpen the mind, and give a background to early Christianity. It would also help to develop the art of rhetoric and an ability to communicate carefully.

The mathematics syllabus in the College dealt with some basic geometry theory, but was largely algebra and arithmetic, and a theological student required considerable ability and appreciation of mathematics to be convinced of its value.

Nevertheless, mathematics could sharpen reasoning powers, encourage conceptual thinking and provide a framework of discipline. It might even prove useful in the practical affairs of a church. Such study was seen as part of the general education required by the student to hold their own in nineteenth-century society.

In biblical studies the College maintained a commitment to linguistic studies and exegesis. Few attempts were made to teach an overall theological knowledge of Old and New Testaments. A conservative institution, such as Spurgeon's, maintained the commitment of Hengstenberg, the Sermon commentary writer, to plenary inspiration and infallibility. Other colleges followed fellow Sermon commentators, de Wette, Gesenius and Neander, in rejecting the theory of verbal inspiration but maintained a deep reverence for the divine authority of the Holy Scriptures. Attempts were made to relate biblical studies to preaching, but the Homerton college practice of allocating a text to students for sermon class was not followed, with the result that students could preach continually from the best known passages of Scripture and neglect the historical books of the Old Testament and the New Testament epistles.

The College taught a natural theology, confidently assuming that this could be worked out by a metaphysical approach. The ordering of systematic material might lack logic and structure, and seem to begin with men rather than with revelation, whilst there was little focus on the historical Jesus, the Holy Spirit or the last things. The rigid, proportional, metaphysical approach of the nineteenth-century was very different from the more dynamic, existential, historical approach of today. The thorough content of the lectures would need an enlivening presentation if they were to stimulate the minds and whet the mental appetites of students enough to make them systematic theologians in ministry, keeping abreast of developments relating to the needs of their congregations. One of the most serious weaknesses of the syllabus was inadequate reference to social trends. Whether students were to minister in urban, rural or overseas settings, they needed help in contextualising their theological study.

The main emphasis was on plenary inspiration, substitutionary atonement and everlasting punishment. Few students were as bright as Spurgeon and so most failed to benefit fully from the intensive instruction at the College. They followed him out of trust, although he hankered after a past era. They ministered in a new one, for which they were insufficiently prepared. The students' respect for Spurgeon and the tutors could lead to blind obedience rather than mature judgement.

The Method of Examination

The earliest available examples of examinations at Spurgeon's College come from 1916. The emphasis is on languages—Hebrew, Greek and Latin. The allocation of marks is defined for each question. Even at this stage all the questions in the Church History paper demand factual material, introduced by What, Give, Who... There is no attempt to use quotations or demand discussion.[12] Academically, Spurgeon's College was far behind the other London colleges, whose teaching methods and examination questions had been profoundly influenced by the university. However, the translation from Hebrew concerns passages of similar difficulty to those used in the late twentieth century, though they are much narrower in scope. The grammar is more demanding, especially in terms of parsing, but the exegesis required is very simple, asking factual questions which demand no more than the learning of lecture notes. The examination reflects no attempt to develop critical faculties or assess current literature or commentaries. The focus is on learning facts rather than developing intellectual abilities. It is interesting to see that the New Testament's usage of the Old Testament is included, but only in terms of learning references, not in theological and hermeneutical development.

Late nineteenth-century debate about examinations in general can clearly be applied to theological colleges.[13] The advantages of an examination system were recognised. Examinations could have a bracing effect on lazy pupils and slipshod teachers. They could provide an objective test of the effectiveness of the teaching and of the students' knowledge. Examinations subjected teachers to external standards and central influences, curbing an arbitrary selection of topics and books for the syllabus. Working for examinations encouraged care, perseverance and concentration, and could be a powerful stimulus to the indolent.

On the other hand, the examination system could be open to abuse, Many contemporary commentators were concerned about examinations leading to financial reward in the form of scholarships or prizes. Some believed that to put a price on knowledge was wrong, and that examinations should not be used to gain advantage or position, or merely for the sake of results. There was a risk that students might lose their individuality as they crammed mechanically for examinations, precluding originality and debasing the value of education and original thought. Others believed that examinations should be qualifying but never competitive, certifying proficiency but proffering no reward, and showing unfitness by failure. Internal, non-competitive examinations could be susceptible to favouritism and lack objectivity in assessing individual progress. Examinations might encourage superficiality, because it did not pay to pursue a subject beyond a certain point. Style could count for more than matter, cleverness for more than depth, a passing acquaintance with many subjects for more than real knowledge of one. Some feared that students could allow themselves to be so motivated to succeed in examinations that wider and deeper interests would be repressed. Much rote-learning could lead to neglect of the rational faculties, with the desire to appear to know rather than to know.

There were particular dangers for theological colleges: those coming top in academic assessments could easily acquire a false view of their professional competence for ministry. Examinations inevitably tested one or two facets rather than the whole person. Their teachers might value them highly as scholars and evaluate them less as prospective pastors. Those not so academically gifted could feel of little worth when it came to professional competence. There was always a risk that students cramming for examinations might not grasp any real understanding of their subject and therefore not be able to communicate it effectively in later years.

They might not be equipped with the skills needed later to tackle new developments not taught at college. Many of the examinations at Spurgeon's College required short, superficial answers to direct, factual questions, so students' minds were directed to factual information, not stimulated to reflection and personal conviction.

As the nineteenth-century drew to its close, there was a growing desire to avoid the worst excesses of the system: consultation among examiners was developed and there was more specialisation and objectivity. In the thirty years following Spurgeon's death, the College gradually laid more emphasis on the teaching gift of ministers and the intellectual activity required to sustain it. Church links diminished, but denominational awareness grew, as residential community training became the pattern.

Contraction

In 1877 the College had 111 students. By 1898 that number had diminished to fifty-seven, and in 1917, at the height of the First World War, the College was temporarily closed for eighteen months as numbers had dwindled to six, after many had volunteered for War service. War apart, the numerical decline had serious consquences for College finances and morale. Even in 1891, when Spurgeon was still alive, there were complaints that the College was producing too many ministers, and the College authorities acknowledged that a number of those trained were not serving in full pastoral charge of churches, but rather as lay preachers, lay pastors or itinerant evangelists.

The great era of Spurgeonic church planting was largely

over and, although many men were going overseas as part of the great missionary enthusiasm of the time, the College had to note what was happening in the market-place. It was repeatedly said that there was no shortage of candidates for the College, but between 1892 and 1922 judicious selection was in operation: 'The Trustees deem it wise not to increase the numbers this year but to wait till the senior men have found spheres of service before any fresh students shall be selected from the hundreds of applicants seeking admission to the College.'[14] Contraction mainly occurred for financial reasons: 'Support from the Tabernacle Church was wonderfully well sustained...but outside support had diminished.'[15] The Annual Report of 1895 contained the first direct appeal for funds[16] promising that the educational standards of the College were being raised. From 4 February 1919 a separate Candidate Committee met twice a month to consider applications. No-one over thirty-three was admitted, nor were married men without financial guarantees for the welfare of their families. Before long the whole College Committee made the selection.

It became increasingly difficult to house the students in the homes of Tabernacle members, partly because of the unsatisfactory nature of some residences, partly because students preferred to make their own arrangements. Anyway the scheme became increasingly difficult to run in a financially viable way. The number of students accepted was clearly made to correspond to the number of lodging houses available, and as no new homes were opened, students were sometimes deferred for a year until accommodation was available. Sadly the contraction was not only in numbers but also in morale.

Rogers and Gracey died at the same time as Spurgeon. This meant a wealth of experience was taken away and a leadership vacuum existed, although Spurgeon's brother, James Archer, became Treasurer and continued as Trustee of the College until his death on March 22 1899. Three years previously Spurgeon's twin sons, Thomas and Charles, became President and Vice-President repectively until the early years of World War I. It was difficult to expect any one of these men to offer the same style and calibre of leadership such as Charles had offered in the early days.[17] In 1908 Archibald Brown was appointed a Vice-President in an attempt to broaden the leadership,[18] but he soon resigned, finding the work too demanding alongside his pastorate.[19]

In the 1890s a small group of Trustees, sometimes as few as four at any given monthly meeting, tried manfully to administer the affairs of a number of organisations which had begun at the zenith of Spurgeon's fame and were now struggling to continue usefully in a different world. A typical monthly agenda included items about the housing and number of students, applications and settlements, chapel applications to the Loan Fund, College finance and fabric, staff matters, and reports on other Spurgeonic organisations, like the Evangelists.[20] The Trustees had to administer the Loan Building Fund, superintend the Pioneer Mission and other evangelistic associations connected with the College, try to assist needy former students in pastorates with continuing education, provide for the widows of ministers, and cope with the daily demands of College life. Many of the Trustees had long been loyal servants of Spurgeon, but they were now elderly and unable to cope with change or offer inspiring leadership when outward circumstances were denting morale.

Fig. 3.1 The Rev. Thomas Spurgeon, the third President of the College 1896–1917.

In 1900 the very successful evening classes, which had been running since the mid-1860s, were closed down. This was mainly because much of the work had been taken over by the polytechnic classes of the London County Council. Nevertheless, the closure was painful, as the end of the Victorian era saw the demise of an enterprising and imaginative aspect of the College's work, which had not only served as a pre-collegiate study course, but had offered training to many Christian young men later engaged in all kinds of Christian work.[20]

Deprivation

Spurgeon had tried to run the College on faith/mission principles, and by his own genius and his influence in the evangelical world, the College's financial needs had been met. Without him the College authorities attempted to maintain the same principles but found it increasingly difficult. The burden of the College work fell more and more onto the Tabernacle funds at a time when its own life was not as healthy as formerly, so more and more time had to be given to fund raising. Even in the late 1890s deficits were recorded annually. Between 1903 and 1909 expenditure exceeded income by over £500 a year. Some years, legacies accounted for nearly half the total income: the College was only saved from financial disaster by legacies which went straight into the General Fund, and by drawing on reserves contingently set aside in healthier years. It became clear that financial factors governed the whole enterprise: salaries, library provision, general maintenance and even the number of students. Such a situation debilitates morale. General contributions fell off, in spite of a winsome appeal: 'We appeal to all who love the truth which Mr Spurgeon so fully and fearlessly preached to aid us to carry on.'[21] A College Jubilee Fund hoped to raise £10,000, but 'our appeal to the public has not as yet met with the response we had hoped for.'[22] 'Consequently, we have no change in policy but the need for funds is greater than ever.'[23]

Because of the financial need the number of trustees was increased to thirteen all able to be active, and the College Conference was asked to elect some of their number as a consultative Committee to offer help and support in meeting the financial needs of the College.

First, specific schemes of fund raising were devised. On

10 February 1910 it was brought to the attention of the Committee that in the years between 1904 and 1909 the average income had been £2,642, while the average cost of students had been £3,336. On 26 May 1910 the Trustees, Pastor and Deacons of the Tabernacle met to consider the financial condition of the College and decided upon a policy of retrenchment in terms of student numbers, saving £45.00 per annum maintenance upon each reduction. Closing the College was contemplated. The Treasurer believed it would cost £8,000 to complete the education of the men already in training; the possibility of borrowing from the Loan Building Fund was to be investigated. Pastor A.G. Brown felt 'that a minister should settle in a church, continuant upon the promise of an annual collection from the members of the Pastors' College.' Professor Gaussen suggested that some incoming students could obtain the names of persons in the sending churches who would subscribe if applied to. Dr McCaig thought that holiday collecting cards could be handed to students willing to take them. Other suggestions included printed lists of annual subscribers who should be reminded when amounts became due, asking pastors to supply the names of members of their churches who might be approached for subscriptions, and application to the Particular Baptist Fund for a yearly contribution. Previous Vice-Presidents of Conference were to be asked to meet with the Trustees in September to advise about future policy and procedure in the raising of funds. In 1910 only £303 15s and 6d had been received from churches;a further £1,000 was needed each year.

The meeting recommended:

i) The desirability of forming an Advisory Council.
ii) The necessity of adopting some means of impressing the churches which are presided over by College men with the importance of the claims of the College.
iii) New financial methods such as a subscription list, deputation work, collecting cards.
iv) The advisability of advertisements setting forth the work and needs of the College.

At a meeting of the College Trustees it was reported that on 13 October 1911 Stockwell Pastors' Trustees, a joint sub-committee of the Orphanage and College, had recommended that Thomas Spurgeon should be appointed a Deputation Worker. The recommendation was adopted but it mainly benefited the Orphanage.[24] On 23 November 1916 the College Conference wrote to the Trustees indicating their willingness to set aside twelve brethren to act with the Trustees and staff as the General Management Committee of the College. It was recognised that the Trustees needed the right of veto over those from Conference. Nominations by any member of the Conference, countersigned by two other members, were to be sent in by the end of January in each year. Of the twelve brethren selected from this list at the first business meeting of the Conference, eight should reside in London in order to secure sufficient, regular attendance. The start of this voluntary service coincided with the resignation of Charles and Thomas Spurgeon whose failing energies were taken up with orphanage work. Sadly the meeting concluded 'that the present circumstances of the College occasioned by War demand the practical suspension of its normal activities.'[25]

At first these elected members of Conference were financial advisors. Gradually, however, regional representation was developed and ideas for regional scholarships to support students evolved. By 1923 the College was governed not by trustees but by an elected Council, consisting of some of the remaining trustees, elected Council members and the College staff. Sub-committees of this Council looked after finance, fabric and other special needs.

The First World War, with its displacement and upheaval, had brought the crisis to a head. In the wake of the war the Chairman of the Council, John Bradford, offered new leadership, and steps were taken to sell the building at the Tabernacle to the London County Council for use as a day school, and purchase a property elsewhere. After unsuccessful attempts to purchase Bessemer House, on Denmark Hill, in Camberwell, the Hay Walker family offered a house, set in eight acres of land in South Norwood, to the College. This gift was conditional upon the continuation of the Spurgeonic basis of faith and the Calvinistic and evangelistic position of the College. Although £25,000 had to be raised to effect the move from Newington Butts to South Norwood and equip the new College, the Hay Walker gift provided the opportunity for a new beginning in a new location with new impetus and a new approach.

Curriculum

Some modifications were now made in the curriculum to increase the academic standing of the College. These included external contacts to discuss the possible entry of students for London University examinations; even the possible participation of the College in London University itself was explored. In 1909 the secretary of the Baptist Union, John Howard Shakespeare, enquired whether the College would be prepared to participate in a central selection process. The federal suggestions were:

i) That every candidate for ministerial training must, in the first instance, approach the College directly which he desires to enter with the recommendation of the church of which he is a member and of the District Council of the locality where he resides.

ii) That a central ministerial education fund shall be formed including representatives of all affiliated colleges under the Baptist Union.

iii) That subject to a candidate being accepted by the College Committee he shall then be examined by the Central Board as to his general fitness for the work of the ministry. If the candidate satisfies the Central Board in this respect he shall then be eligible to sit for the entrance examination of the College for which he has applied.

These proposals were vehemently rejected by Spurgeon's college trustees who asserted their independence within an overall commitment to the work of the Union. The minutes declare 'that the Trustees would never agree to any scheme which would in any way interfere with their absolute and sole authority in the matter of the choice and training of the students of the Pastors' College.'[25]

Evidence from 1916 indicates that although internal examinations were then held twice as year, they still basically

Fig. 3.2 Council, staff and students, 1922.

asked students factual questions which implied rote learning and did not equip independent minds with tools to think for themselves. In the fast changing world following the devastation of the First World War, this was not a healthy educational or training exercise. Meanwhile, students were asking for changes in the curriculum, and adjustments were made to the timetable to include such new subjects as Pastoral Theology and Psychology. On 11 June 1919 a group of students was received by the Committee. They sought:

i) the appointment of a Deputation Secretary;
ii) the abolition of college houses;
iii) the provision of post-collegiate courses;
iv) a change in the mode of electing college committees;
v) a revision of the curriculum with:

- greater facilities for degree courses in connection with the University;
- inclusion of such subjects as Sociology, Comparative Religion and Science;
- extension of curriculum in Pastoral Theology, Biblical Instruction and Psychology;
- rearrangement in regard to the Thursday discussion class;
- adoption of new text books.[26]

On 15 April 1920 a report was given upon possible affiliation to the University of London. Some members of the staff felt this was desirable in order to raise academic standards. Others felt it would limit the College's ability to offer courses to students of widely differing educational backgrounds.

On 25 January 1924 a sub-committee report was received on the curriculum. Whilst it appeared impossible to eliminate any of the current subjects from the curriculum, the addition of others was considered desirable. A course of five Friday lectures on pastoral theology had been arranged and the committee recommended that such subjects as sociology and Bible study work in Sunday schools and amongst young people, as well as pastoral theology, should be dealt with systematically by lecturers on Friday afternoons. The Committee discussed the complaint that students were overburdened and made the following recommendations:

i) that fewer and shorter business meetings be held;
ii) that the following exemptions be granted: junior men from Church History, middle men from Pastoral Theology, third year men from Hebrew;

iii) that tutors be asked to consult with the wardens and students as to the possibility of having the evening prayers immediately after tea. It would then be possible for men to commence an uninterrupted evening's work at six o'clock.
iv) the Committee regard it as undesirable for student pastors to be attending any week evening meetings in their churches.[27]

On 25 March 1920 the Council were asked whether the Pastors' College would open its door to female students to take its theological course. Mr Greenwood, the Chairman, pointed out that the Trust Deeds specifically stated that the College was for the training of young men for the ministry, that none of the funds of the College could be used for any other purpose, but that the admittance of women to some of the lectures would not be contrary to the spirit of the Trustees as long as they entailed no expense to the College and did not deflect funds from their legitimate and special work of training young men.[28]

Staff

Through this period the work was mainly in the hands of Archibald McCaig and W.H. Gaussen. McCaig was born at Bridge of Earn, near Perth, on 31 March 1852 and spent his boyhood at Cowdenbeath, Fife. From the beginning he was an eager scholar, but his father's sudden death compelled him to leave school to support the home. At the age of sixteen he was converted, and immediately started to preach, but a cautious Presbyterian minister stirred up a prosecution against him and some of his comrades. They were found guilty, but discharged with a caution on the grounds that 'they were under the delusion that they were preaching the gospel.' Conversions followed such preaching, however, and study of the New Testament led to the little company of converts adopting Baptist principles. A Baptist church was formed, and Archibald McCaig was chosen as first pastor. In 1876 he married Sarah MacDiarmid Offock. The way opened for him to serve as colporteur-pastor at Offord D'Arcy and Buckden in Huntingdonshire, and this in turn led to his admission to Spurgeons College in 1881. After work as student-pastor at Lewin Road, Streatham, he moved to Brannoxtown, Ireland, where his ardent scholarship earned him the degrees of BA, LLB and then LLD, at Queen's University, Belfast. In 1892 he returned to Spurgeon's College, where for a third of a century he taught, having no fewer than 474 ministers and missionaries as his pupils. From 1898 to 1925 he was Principal, and on his retirement was made Principal-Emeritus. Dr McCaig was deeply interested in evangelistic work on the continent, particularly in Russia, and his travels and extraordinary linguistic gifts made him of great use to such enterprise. He possessed a wonderful memory, a passion for knowledge, and a reverent love of truth, coupled with tenderness and fidelity. As a theologian he bowed before the majesty of revelation, and his chief writings were in defence of Biblical inspiration.

For forty-five years McCaig was associated with the College, which he loved. He was devoted to it not merely by official position, but by profound love for C.H. Spurgeon, ardent faith in the gospel Spurgeon preached, and brotherly affection for all the College students. His gifts were only partly known to the outside world, for he hid the workman in the work, but over the years the worth of his teaching was revealed in the lives of his students. For thirty years he was Secretary of the Conference, and President in 1926. One of his early Conference Addresses spoke of 'The Cross as the Inspiration of Christian Service,' and he gloried in that Cross throughout his eighty-five years.

The oversight of James Archer Spurgeon proved an important bridge into the twentieth century. During his student days at Stepney he acquired a reputation as a brilliant preacher; and in his studies proved so keen a scholar that few could rival him as a linguist. It was his reputation as a scholar in Syriac and cognate languages, as well as his long service at the Tabernacle, that was later recognised in the award of two honorary degrees from American universities.

McCaig and James Spurgeon were great leaders, but were still really representatives of the nineteenth rather than the emerging twentieth century. It was left to Percy Evans to give the post-war College new impetus.

A New Building

This period of transition during which the leadership of the College spread out from one man to embrace his family and the leadership of the Church of which he had been the Pastor, was followed by the establishment of a College Council. This had limited Spurgeonic representation and even the influence of the Tabernacle declined. It became more and more difficult for students living at a distance to attend the Monday night prayer meeting at the Tabernacle. Participation in the life and work of the Church decreased as students were encouraged to give more and more time to their studies. In their earnestness they wanted to devote the hours to study and not simply to participation in the life of the Tabernacle or to practical exercises. Eventually the move in 1923 made the College residential and altered the character, ethos, atmosphere and outlook of those who trained there.

In 1874 Mr Spurgeon had erected the buildings at the rear of the Tabernacle, for tuition only, with students boarded nearby. In time men had to be housed as far away as Woolwich, Stratford and Stoke Newington; whilst the noise around the buildings hampered instruction.[29]

With these difficulties in mind in April 1921 the College Council appointed a committee 'to arrange for visits to the students in their various houses; and to have before them the securing of a house suitable for a Residential College.' For the next year this committee looked into various premises and then came the exciting news: 'Mr Bradford reported that Mr Hay Walker would give us Falkland House and six or eight acres of land on certain conditions that would be acceptable. The Doxology was sung with much fervour and gratitude.'[30]

Falkland House was eminently suitable. An earlier Estate Agent's brochure described it as: 'Occupying a unique position on the summit of South Norwood Hill, overlooking an extraordinary panorama of scenery extending to seven counties...yet being situated within half-an-hour's motor ride of the City and West End. The Crystal Palace is one mile distant. Containing some twenty-eight Bed and Dressing Rooms...the property is installed with the electric light.'[31]

Named after the first owner Admiral the Hon. Plantagenet Pierrepoint Carey, eleventh Viscount Falkland, the

Fig. 3.3 *Left:* Professor W.H. Gaussen, MA, LLB (1898–1938); *Centre:* Principal A. McCaig, BA, LLD (1898–1925); *Right:* Professor P.W. Evans, BA, BD (1902–1925).

magnificent mansion originally stood in nearly thirty acres of park and woodland. From the gate-house at the top of the hill, the drive wound down through oak, chestnut and ash trees. A large conservatory, 265 feet long hot house, stabling, cottages and a 'model hand laundry' were all on the estate. Following the death of his wife, Fanny Walker, Mr Charles Hay Walker proposed to give the house and some of the surrounding land to the Trustees of the Pastors' College. The remaining land was sold off for development into private houses.

At last the right premises were available and only half a mile away from Spurgeon's home 'Westwood', on Beulah Hill; but the Council faced the enormous task of altering and equipping the building for its new role: a task made even more difficult by the current deficit. An appeal was launched to raise £25,000, a large figure for the 1920s. '...renovations, the making of a new road, fencing and furnishing, will cost not much less than £5,000, the rest is required to meet rates, maintenance of the buildings, and other expenses which the ordinary income of the College is insufficient to meet.'[32]

The trust deeds were signed in June 1922. 'The only condition attached to its use being that the doctrines so dear to the heart of C.H. Spurgeon, and always associated with the teaching of the College, should be maintained.'[33] With half the appeal figure met, the decision was formally taken to occupy the new house from August 1923. The garage, laundry and one cottage were sub-let. A gardener was employed and an extra strip of land was bought to provide a new drive. Under the supervision of the Wardens, The Rev. and Mrs H.M. Greenwood, preparations went ahead: drawing room was transformed into lecture hall, assorted bedrooms, dressing rooms and servants quarters became study-bedrooms. The entrance hall took on a new look. On Monday 20 August the students arrived in time for five o'clock tea.

The Sword and the Trowel, reported the opening:

> 'The new session of the College began on 21 August in the new building, Falkland Park, henceforth to be known as Spurgeon's College. Ten new students were welcomed by the Chairman, Mr Bradford, four of whom are Missionary candidates. In the morning a prayer meeting was held and then tutors and students went into the Class Rooms, the Common Room, Dining Room, Office and Warden's Room, and one Student's Bedroom as representative of all: and had a short religious exercise by way of "dedicating" each room.'[34]

Fig. 3.4 South view—Spurgeon's College (1922).

The formal Public Opening was held on 18 December. By then both students and tutors were enjoying a greater fellowship in the new surroundings. The practical arrangements were running smoothly. The Matron's Petty Cash Book for the first ten terms shows the variety of minor expenses incurred: everything from curtain hooks to seven and sixpence worth of kippers!

Principal McCaig wrote in his Annual Report for 1923:

'The situation is ideal, the accommodation is ample, the management leaves nothing to be desired. The home life...cannot fail to be helpful: the time saved from hours spent travelling to and fro is utilised to great advantage.'[35]

A new era had begun.

CHAPTER 4

The Brethren
1923–1957

THE SPURGEON TRADITION, in its commitment to the Bible, Jesus, the cross, the gospel and soul-winning, has emerged in many different kinds and varieties of ministers. The College in the twentieth century has been able to train a wide variety of people for the varying Christian ministries, but all grounded in the tradition which Spurgeon began.

A former student, W.R. Chesterton, expressed his view of the College tradition:

> Here then is this Spurgeon tradition, a tradition peculiarly associated with the College, a tradition that gives the place of honour to the pioneers and the evangelist, a tradition that sent men out to make churches and not merely minister to those made for them. It is not the Spurgeon tradition that a man should be uncouth, undisciplined, uneducated or ungentlemanly, either in mind or appearance. That does not make him a suitable evangelist. It is the Spurgeon tradition that all a man's gifts inherited and acquired should be baptised in the passion of the soul winner.[1]

The Community

Although the 1920s saw continuing links between the College and the Spurgeon family, the old ties were gradually lessening. The establishment of the College at Falkland Park heralded not only a new era but a new ethos, since the College was now a residential community. On 27 January 1927 the College Council remembered the death of Charles Spurgeon Jnr. and recorded its gratitude for his life of service to the College. On 26 March 1925 the Council had approached Harold Spurgeon, Principal of the Dublin Bible College, to join the staff, but without success. In spite of these continuing links with the founder, a new dimension of college life was opening up after the turmoil of the First World War. There are still living witnesses to the life of the College between 1923 and 1957, so it is possible to give a more animated account of those formative years, relying not only on the formal records, but also on eye-witness accounts, beginning with the application procedures.

Application Procedures

The formal selection process was clear. The prospective student made a written request to be considered and was then required to fill in a schedule of questions, which included: 'The cost of your training will be £50 per year for four years. What can your church and friends contribute towards this amount?' The returned schedule had to be supported by the signatures of the pastor and church secretary of the applicant's home church and approved by the corporate gathering of the church meeting. The applicant also had to supply the names and addresses of three well-known Christian workers who had been intimately acquainted with him for at least two years and from whom reference could be sought. One of these had to be his minister and two must have heard the applicant preach. The applicant also had to submit a fully-written sermon of his own composition, a medical form indicating good health, and a promise to undertake the pre-collegiate study scheme which included preliminary Greek, Latin and English Grammar, and an acquaintance with the books of the Bible. Specific books were set for study such as Matthew's Gospel and the Acts of the Apostles. Successful applicants were called for interview. These interviews with the full College Council lasted half an hour.

In 1927 seventy initial applications were received and, of these, thirty were sent schedules and considered as serious applicants. Six were declined, seven were invited to re-apply after further experience, and seventeen were invited for interview by the College Council. Most applicants were destined for Baptist ministry either at home or overseas, but some applied to be preachers of the gospel with other organisations, such as the Spanish Gospel Mission. It was generally recognised that an applicant's call should be to a lifelong ministry of preaching. He needed both evangelistic zeal and an ability to work hard. No one was accepted over the age of twenty-five. Quite a number of students were from a Brethren, rather than a Baptist, background.

The College wished to train men to become attractive, effective preachers of the gospel and good expositors of Scripture—evangelists and missionaries who could bear the brunt of the battle in pioneering work. In selecting such men, the Council was guided by several considerations. Applicants should be between twenty-one and twenty-five years of age, unmarried, and preferably not engaged to marry. They should show an aptitude for sustained intellectual work, and had to produce evidence that they had preached the gospel frequently for at least two years. The seal of the Holy Spirit upon such preaching, as evidenced by the winning of souls to Christ, was of the utmost importance. Every student was required to contribute according to his ability towards the cost of his maintenance whilst in college, though lack of means was not an insuperable barrier to admission. Clear conviction of the call of God to the work outweighed every other requirement. The theological position of the College was 'the faith once for all delivered to the saints'. The College opposed all who questioned verbal inspiration, devalued the Atonement, and rationalised the supernatural forces of Christianity. It stood by the Bible, the cross of Christ, the new birth and the blessed hope. Those of different persuasion would be out of harmony with the spirit of the College, and should not apply for admission.

S.J. Dewhurst, tutor from 1955 to 1979, stressed the importance of

> 'A personal experience of the salvation that is in Christ; the acceptance, by the applicant, of Christ's Lordship over his life; and a desire to bear witness to others concerning His redeeming love.'[2]

Another tutor wrote an imaginary letter to an enquirer:

> 'We are quickly moving into an age wherein a man must have qualifications from a recognised body in order to gain a hearing from those who are outside the orbit of the Church. Many of the

young people in your church in the future will have passed the new General Certificate of Education and you should strive to have at least that minimum educational qualification. It may be that you are engaged in technical studies or are apprenticed to a trade—then you should complete those studies or apprenticeship, for you do not know of what value they may be to you in the ministry.'[3]

The same tutor addressed the problem of selection:

'The fundamental question upon which the Council must be wholly satisfied is whether a man has received a call from God to preach. Having assured ourselves, then, that the candidate has indeed been called to preach, and having heard of the effects of his preaching (for we demand that a man shall have been preaching for at least two years), we seek then to find an answer to the question whether the candidate is thereby called to the full-time ministry. Many questions arise, therefore, as we seek to assess whether the call of God is to be exercised in business or in the full-time ministry. There is the question of health—can a man stand the rigours of the pastoral life? Again, there is the question of ability to live with one's fellow man. He has to minister to a beloved community—beloved, but growing into the love of God, and at times the tensions of growth and the passions still unredeemed are evident.'[4]

The interviews with the College Council all took place at the Metropolitan Tabernacle and were a terrifying ordeal before a venerable company of men. In 1925 the College Council launched a scheme which tried to raise twenty sums of £500 each, yielding exhibitions of £25 a year towards the £90 cost of a student's course. These were to be distributed on an area basis, with three reserved for missionaries and four in the gift of individuals. By 1928 only £1,712 had been received

CONCERNING ADMISSION TO THE COLLEGE

Many years ago the aim of the College was clearly indicated by C. H. Spurgeon in the following sentences: —

" We desire to train men to become attractive, impressive, effective preachers of the Gospel. We want them also to be good expositors of Scripture. We much desire to see a host of true Pastors as the result of the College training. We long to see born in this College a considerable number of evangelists and missionaries ; wherever a man is wanted to bear the brunt of the battle, let a brother from the College be forthcoming."

The intervening years have only served to stress the wisdom of our great leader. In the endeavour to discharge the responsible task of selecting such men, the Council is guided by several considerations.

1.—It is too large an enterprise to train workers or more than one denomination. **Only those are accepted who are called to exercise their ministry in connection with Baptist Churches or Missions.** Applicants should be between 21 and 25 years of age, unmarried, and preferably not engaged.

2.—No College can make a preacher, and evidence is required in each case that the applicant has been engaged in preaching the Gospel frequently for at least two years, before his application can be considered. The definite seal of the Holy Spirit upon such preaching, as evidenced by the winning of souls to Christ, is of the utmost importance.

3.—Every Student is required to contribute according to his ability towards the cost of his maintenance whilst in College, though lack of means is not an insuperable barrier to admission. Clear conviction of the call of God to the work outweighs every other requirement.

4.—If the above considerations are dominant, no rigidly uniform standard of scholarship can be applied to applicants, yet an educated ministry was never more needed than to-day. A preliminary course of study is therefore prescribed, and each candidate selected for interview must satisfy the College Council, both orally *and by previous written examination*, that he has worked conscientiously through this course, that he has utilised his opportunities to the full, and that he has an aptitude for serious and sustained intellectual work.

5.—The theological position of the College has been well summarised by one of her sons. He says :—

" The College stands by ' the faith once for all delivered to the saints,' and is the declared foe of all who minimise Inspiration, slight the Atonement, and rationalise the supernatural forces of Christianity. It stands by the Book of God, the Cross of Christ, the New Birth and the Blessed Hope."

Those who differ from this statement would be out of harmony with the spirit of the College, and it would be wise for such not to apply for admission.

6.—The College course extends to at least four years. The first session is regarded strictly as a probationary period, and all students are admitted upon this understanding. New students enter in the autumn, and **all applications must be to hand by December 31st of the preceding year.**

7.—Further information will be forwarded on receipt of a stamped addressed envelope. All correspondence should be addressed in the first instance to The Secretary, Spurgeon's College, South Norwood Hill. S.E.25.

Fig. 4.1 Application: concerning admission to the college.

for the exhibition, but it was moderately successful in helping to put college finances on a secure basis and providing some help for people whose personal and church resources were limited.

Corporate Activity

When the College moved in 1923, many of the newly resident men had just returned from war. They were worldly wise, while their tutors tended to be classical men rather detached from the real world. Only the senior students had a room of their own. Most stayed for three years and in their second year would normally share with three or four other students. In the first year some shared rooms but others had to be billeted with families in the South Norwood church. The College fellowship became an enriching experience where lasting friendships were formed. Students learned to cultivate the devotional and spiritual life and acquired habits of study which continued in the discipline of the pastorate. Indeed the close fellowship of about forty men from many backgrounds and different parts of the country was in itself a preparation for ministry.

College life had its incidents and excitements, its difficulties and challenges, its serious work and boisterous fun. Ragging was frequent and sometimes injudicious. Being an all male community, it was a safety valve and relaxation after serious study. It could afford healthy exercise in self-control amid the thrust and parry of student life. Student meetings could be forthright and pugnacious, but grace would prevail: the abiding memory of most former students is one of beneficial fellowship. Facilities were frugal and puritan, but the conditions drove the students to seek inward strength. There was a good deal of formality, students either being addressed as 'gentlemen' or by their surnames. There was a clear hierarchy among the students, but a great sense of brotherhood. Each yearly intake formed a 'batch' which did most things together, encouraging loyalty and pride. Batch prayer meetings were held twice a week and there was a full college prayer meeting on Friday afternoons, devoted to the preaching and student pastoral activities of the weekend. Each morning the Principal took morning prayers for students and domestic staff. After breakfast, lectures and classes were held from 9.15 until 12.45. Following lunch at 1.00 the afternoon was free, with the Principal encouraging students to participate in sport or some other exercise or personal hobby. Sport played a large part in student life, with college football and cricket teams playing other theological colleges. There were also internal tournaments, in tennis, table tennis and darts. Between 6.00 and 10.00pm strict silence was maintained for private study or preparation for the next day's classes, apart from a half hour break for supper. There were no evening prayers. All students had to undertake two hours a week gardening in the eight acres of grounds.

The whole of college life was bonded together, not merely subdivided. Student administration was democratically centred in the students' Common Room. Negotiations with the tutors were transacted through a Student Chairman and six senior students called 'Apostles', who formed an executive committee. All decisions were ratified by all the students in Common Room business sessions and the Apostles were elected by the whole body of students in collaboration with the Principal and tutors. The Student Chairman's responsibility included leading regular business meetings, serving as Secretary of the Apostles' meetings, presiding at Common Room communion services, receiving and presiding over meetings with them, representing the students to the Principal and effecting all decisions made by the students.

Most men possessed only one good suit, reserved for weekend speaking engagements. In college they wore shabby, shiny old outfits. Money was in short supply. Most men lived on or near the poverty line, having no regular source of income for four years. As far as possible they met college fees, and gave of their own skills in college life, e.g. a qualified electrician made a vast improvement in the lighting and heating of the building.

College terms fell mainly in the cooler months. In term time the building was heated, but tutors sometimes wore overcoats while lecturing when the weather was especially cold.

Students' rooms needed auxiliary heating by gas fires, which had an insatiable appetite for shillings in the meter. Often dressing-gowns were worn over normal clothes and legs were wrapped in ex-army blankets. The three meals a day were plain, wholesome and sufficient, although they lacked variety and barely satisfied youthful appetites. Food parcels from home were not uncommon. After vacations students were often seen struggling up the College drive with two suitcases, one filled with clean laundry and the other with food. Weekend preaching occasions were a welcome respite from the somewhat Spartan existence, for they not only gave a glimpse of ministry but supplied preaching fees, good food and comfortable hospitality.

The Whitehouse Missionary Fellowship, named after the

Fig. 4.2 First resident students, tutors and wardens (1923).

first College missionary martyr in China, was very active. The Missionary Study Circle invigorated interest in overseas mission, as the students, fresh from earlier study and thought, came in a spirit of prayer and spiritual keenness. Visiting speakers compelled the students to widen their horizons and informed them about the wider Christian world. The programme included the study of Kenneth Maclennan's book, *The Cost of a New World*—and the students discussed questions of missionary programme and policy based upon a Student Christian Movement Questionnaire.'[5]

The student magazine of the 1920s offered an animated defence of student pastoral service at home:

'The Student Pastorate is viewed in some quarters with undisguised enmity. It is said to cause a division of interest in the life of the student and to require his giving to the work of the pastorate time that should be devoted to study. This seems, however, to ignore the fact that men enter college not primarily to study, but to become equipped for the great work of the Christian ministry. Study is useful in so far as it is a means to that end, but it is by no means the only requirement of the student. The work of a Student Pastorate can often provide him with as much equipment in certain directions as the College curriculum provides in others. From my own knowledge of its advantages, I am of the opinion that all students would benefit immeasureably by sharing them.

Through the regular, bi-monthly visits to one church, a man is kept in vital touch with the actual life and activity of a Christian Fellowship, and is thereby delivered from the dry, arid experiences which, admittedly, are so frequent in normal college life. Moreover, he gains some experience of the actual work of the pastorate, not only of its business side, but of pastoral visitation, and thereby is able to correct false ideas of the ministerial office, which are so easily acquired in College. Then, too, sermon preparation becomes essential, and a man escapes the danger of 'living' on a few sermons, whilst he finds that he can anticipate his later work to the extent of giving progressive, systematic teaching from the pulpit. Really he becomes equipped for the work of the ministry by doing the work of the ministry, for the Student Pastorate offers the same kind of help to the theological student that the operating theatre offers to the medical student.

Nor is the student alone benefited. A church that is unable to support a regular minister is able nevertheless to have someone around whom its members can gather, to whom they may look for leadership. It gains, too, by the progressive character of its pulpit ministry and, further, in having a pastor who is able to help in times of sickness and sorrow, one who is able to supply that personal touch upon which so much depends'[6]

Management and Material Resources

The Hay Walker home, turned college, was a splendid, handsome building in which it was a privilege for students to live. In those days, unencumbered by an accumulation of other ancillary buildings, it commanded wonderful views uninterrupted in all directions. There was no library, no cloister accommodation, no chapel, no Principal's house. These facilities began to be added in the mid 1930s through the generosity of American Baptists when cloister accommodation was added.

In the early 1950s the library was pruned and re-classified. It was decided to budget £100 per year for new purchases. A further £1,000 was raised to purchase books in New Testament literature and theology as a memorial to Percy Evans. An unexpected addition to the library came from the British Council of Churches, after friends in Europe sent theological works to the BCC to form the nucleus of an Ecumenical Library. These works are partly theological and partly exegetical, mainly in German, French and Dutch, although a few, published in Scandinavia, are in English.[7]

On 4 October 1957 the College Chapel was opened at a service of dedication and thanksgiving. In 1946 the Rev. G.W. Harte had first put forward the idea of a chapel. Clifford Measday designed a building specifically for worship in the tradition of the Free Churches, to harmonise with the main suite of buildings.[8]

The house still bore unmistakable signs of its family background in design, decor, and equipment. Public events centred on the hall and main staircase. The Student Common Room, with comfortable armchairs and benches, was used for House Meetings on student affairs, for business and prayer meetings, the Whitehouse Missionary Fellowship, communion services, talks from visiting speakers and daily prayer breakfasts. There were three lecture rooms, the largest, the 'Desk Room', was used for assemblies of the whole student body for Sermon Class, examinations, visiting lecturers and elocution instruction.

Fig. 4.3 Chapel stone-laying.

The College grounds provided opportunity for leisure, relaxation and recreation. There was well-kept woodland with masses of shrubs, such as azaleas and rhododendrons. Springtime brought great areas of primroses, daffodils and narcissi. Walks in the woods served to cool the fevered brow between lectures, study and examinations. Pleasant lawnsafforded room for football and cricket practice, as well as a croquet course. A large, well-tended kitchen garden provided

Fig. 4.4 The College chapel.

Fig. 4.5 A quiet place.

vegetables for the students, whilst a college vinery provided grapes which were sold on Speech Days for college funds. The student cycle shed housed their main means of transport.

The pattern of college life was obviously interrupted by World War Two. During the blitz students brought mattresses down from their rooms and slept on the hall floor. Rooms were cold, and ration books were handed over to Matron, but she gave each student his own sugar ration. Double summertime during the War meant that it was not dark until 11pm, but black-out had to be strictly observed. First aid lessons were given to all students and for a year many served some nights as orderlies at Croydon Hospital.

From 1928 the Council had met quarterly and superintended all of college life. On 22 November that year, council gave approval to the publication of the *College Record*. When students left college they had to gain the approval of the Chairman to settle, which shows that the College was really run by the Council, not just by the Principal and staff. Weekly staff meetings were held, but only lasted an hour; nearly all the business was conducted through committees and sub-committees of the Council.

In the years between the Wars, cordial relationships between the College and the Tabernacle continued, although there was friction over the unsold college buildings which the Council were still discussing in 1926. Student experience of association, union and missionary society life was limited, although many students of this era went with the Baptist Missionary Society to India, China and Africa. Relationships between the College and Baptist Union were cordial, although friction occurred in the 1920s over the Union's medical requirements for ministerial students. They were concerned about pension liabilities. The Council pointed out that over the years several students with fragile health had engaged in effective ministries. The most difficult controversy which threatened the College's relationship with the Union occurred in 1931. After the Downgrade Controversy of 1888, when Spurgeon seceded from the Union, a significant body of Baptist opinion remained sympathetic to him and did not feel that justice had been seen to be done. A strong body of Spurgeonic Baptist life continued, wary of liberal theology and stressing the evangelical hallmarks of biblical inspiration and personal conversion, the saving power of the blood of Christ shed in sacrificial substitutionary atonement and the Second Advent.

Fig. 4.6 Entrance Hall—when occupied by the donor, C. Hay Walker.

In 1931 T.R. Glover wrote a booklet called *Fundamentals* at the request of the Baptist Union. It provoked opposition from those who wanted to challenge Glover's contention that the mystery of the Cross was unfathomable and to present a more traditional view of the atonement. It was agreed that Percy Evans, the Principal of Spurgeon's College, should write a booklet representing the traditional view, and controversy seemed to have been avoided. However, *The Times* had been running a series of articles from various contributors under the title 'Fifty Years', reviewing developments in different fields of activity. Glover was asked to contribute a piece on the Free Churches. He had written it some time in February and it was sheer unfortunate chance that it appeared on 11 March 1932, the Friday of the week in which the Council met. Worse, it was headlined 'The Defeat of Spurgeon', an eye-catching but provocative piece of sub-editing. The main theme was the involvement of the Free Churches in higher and theological education and the influence of Nonconformity in the ancient universities since the abolition of religious tests. Glover went on to argue that British Baptists' attitude to modern learning had been represented and secured by the Baptist Union's stand against Spurgeon's accusations in the Downgrade Controversy. Glover wrote that Spurgeon

> ...had a huge congregation, which in spite of faults of his own and constant criticisms by outsiders, he held charmed. Nature had given him a squat, ugly exterior and made amends by adding a marvellous voice and the supreme gift of oratory. He was an untrained man without the discipline of ordered study, but he read enormously and remembered. Everyone knows how often Catholic and Calvinist have been able to live in the profoundest sense of God's love while holding tenets which others found strangely incompatible with the central belief. Spurgeon was of this stamp. A large hearted, human creature he maintained an Orphanage, and in a rather amateur way he trained young men for the Baptist ministry. It was unhappily no strange thing that a man who attempts too much would prefer at least the homage and tattle of admirers to challenge from independent minds.[9]

Glover gave a racy account of the Downgrade Controversy. Spurgeon alleged that Baptists were abandoning the Bible. After this withdrawal he carried on a tirade against the Union. Glover continued:

> 'I remember asking the aged Frederick Trestral, who in old age kept a clear head and a lively humour, if he thought the trouble came from Spurgeon's gout. "No", he said abruptly. "It was Satan."[10] Well, gout, conscience and Satan make queer alliances in us all. The thing was not done in a corner. The whole Protes-

tant world watched and the Baptists bore the brunt of it. The Controversy in its outcome showed, that Baptists were not crude, unlettered ranters despised by Matthew Arnold. They had trained leaders from their own colleges, university colleges and the Scottish universities. Less famous and less gifted than Spurgeon they nevertheless had a wider intellectual outlook than he.'

The article provoked a response from the minister of the Metropolitan Tabernacle, Tydeman Chilvers, who preached the triumph of Spurgeon and the overthrow of Glover. Next morning a summary of the address appeared in *The Times*. It was in this context that Percy Evans provided an ameliorating influence. Having both the confidence of the Metropolitan Tabernacle and the friendship of Glover, he prevented a wider crisis and eventually brought the College back into membership of the Union in 1938.

The College has been unkindly described as the 'Dr Barnardo's' of theological colleges. Its life was characterised by prayer. Classes began with prayer. On Friday afternoons batteries were recharged and weekend preaching engagements commended at a prayer meeting, and on Sunday mornings those who were not out preaching gathered to pray for those who were. During these inter-War years however, the College developed not only a deep spiritual life but a growing academic reputation, thanks largely to the efforts of the staff.

Staff

One student, Haywood, said of the tutors, 'There are no grinding taskmasters forcing us to delve in murky minds in quest of gems of knowledge. One regards them as mountain guides who lead us ever upward from peak to peak, and at each higher ascent disclosing new vistas of truth to the wandering mind.'[11]

In the twenties the three tutors gave students three times as much work as they could manage, forgetting that most of them were back in school after many years of absence. Percy Evans, the Principal, made the work-load palatable with humour. He came to class one Thursday morning having read the *Church Times*, saying 'Gentlemen, if the angels in heaven read the *Church Times* they must be smiling this morning.' A student asked, 'Sir, what happens when they read the *Baptist Times*?' 'There was silence in heaven for about the space of half an hour' was the reply.[12] Students argued with Mr Gaussen about the value of Latin for theological students, but he was the perfect Christian gentleman, whilst absent-minded Professor Taviner, who once appeared in class clasping the clothes-brush from his hall-stand instead of his Hebrew Bible, was a character loved by all. Students adored him, and his eccentricities. Taviner taught Hebrew, Classical Greek and Philosophy. 'Tavvy' as he was affectionately known, sometimes had to telephone the College from a London railway station, having left some papers at home and forgotten where he was preaching for the day. He could be side tracked by artfully contrived student questions which would make him lay aside Galloway's *Philosophy of Religion* and expound his own. He was a ready speaker. He would get up with apparently no preparation and give an address well put together and sparkling with good things. He never left the Spurgeon theology in which he had been trained, and combined with a philosophical mind the simple faith of earlier years. It was rather difficult, however, to tell where he stood as he had the

Fig. 4.7 Principal Percival Evans, BA, DD (1925–1950).

irritating habit of arguing against almost anything that was said. He had apparently little ambition and loved the quiet life, content with his garden, his dog, his book, and, his pipe. Had he sought greater things for himself he might have found them, but he shunned, rather than courted, any prominent position and was happy among his students, and in occasional ministry to the Churches as an acceptable supply. The warden was D. Russell-Smith, who instructed the first-year students in English Language and Literature, Ancient History and Bible Background, using the *Bible Handbook* by Joseph Angus. He was a better warden than tutor and not as widely popular as the other three.

W.H. Gaussen was scholarly, lovable and approachable. His subjects were mainly Logic, Latin, Psychology and Ethics. An encourager of the slower student, he could even make the dry bones of Logic and Latin live. He could quell and master well-meaning student leg-pulling with a sharp yet gentle wit. One student in the early 1930s found an unlocked drawer in Mr Gaussen's desk and was rude enough to look through the contents. Finding some lecture and lesson notes which bore all the signs of long use, he cheekily added some words from the Prodigal Son's brother: 'Lo, these many years have I served thee.' Next day when the class assembled, Gaussen read the notes and very quietly quoted from Isaiah: 'Gentlemen, even the ass knoweth his Master's crib.' He was held in high regard.

A student remembered Gaussen in the *College Record:*

'A brother beloved, thus we of that earlier breed of students esteemed him, for he had the creative ability of evoking and giving love. He was never sentimental in the lesser meaning of that ambiguous word but his whole nature was made for affection of the finest kind. The feeling that he called forth was in part due to the fact that he was one of the most selfless of men, a trait which both home and religion created in him. There lay his bigness and from out of it emerged his deep interest in each member of his classes. He cared for them as personalities in their own right.

The first impression he made upon a student entering college was of one tall and broad, in perfect proportion, and step and voice were in accord. He never strove for effect but made it by being himself in conscience and heart and spirit. To see him stride into the class-room created its own influence, since what he was in physique he was in character, in mentality, in spirituality, and into his work he brought his total personality.

There was ever a wholeness about him, and probably he would not have won the esteem he did year by year had that sense of deep unity been lacking. With that largeness, grounded in strength, went a marked gentleness of demeanour, characteristic of one who is innately a gentleman, especially God's gentleman.

The tenets of extreme Calvinism were foreign to his heart, and under the test of the gospel he sifted it to the marrow. The judgement of his heart seemed to square with the insight he had of his Master, hence he took from Calvinism what he considered appropriate and left the rest alone. His preaching, therefore, was wide in its range, reasoned and urgent in an appeal for decision, and the churches he served bless his name and memory. He was at home in his Greek New Testament and with the logic of the schools he knew so well, and in the love of his heart and the awe of his spirit, he preached the redeeming Word to all who would heed.

There was thus a certain catholicity about him that drew one to him, and it meant much both in college days and afterwards. Narrowness was impossible to him, either of word or spirit. Because of that wideness of vision and depth of personal committal, he was tolerant, as far as possible, of the debatable positions of others, being so sure of his own standing in Christ. At that time, there were heresies abroad, striving hard for the consent of the leaders of the churches and their members. Many, on a slender acquaintance with the best theology, inflamed large sections of all the churches, sundering not a few from former allegiances. Tempers ran high and voices were strident but he was as one who listened to 'the still small voice' and remained firm upon the truth that had won his earlier response and homage. I cannot recall a single inflammatory word uttered by him and when he spoke on these divisive issues—and we did get him so to do in lecture hours!—it was with marked effect.'[13]

Percy Evans was the best scholar of the faculty, a shrewd judge of character, totally organised, alert and an impressive teacher. Wise and humorous, he was a fatherly and kind man to students in particular need, but would have no undisciplined nonsense or student lethargy. His main sub-

jects were New Testament Greek, Theology, Church History, Homiletics and Pastoral Theology. He was on his own admission a middle-of-the-road man. The academic life and work of the College owed much to his Principalship. His morning prayers were a benediction, reverent, enlightening, inspiring, down-to-earth—a splendid overture to the opening day. A capable theologian, Evans found little time to write because he was devoted to the College. He lectured for approximately sixteen hours a week on a wide range of subjects. He made wise comments at the Sermon Class, expounded the New Testament with depth and was known for the spirituality of his prayers. Evans received an honorary DD after a colleague Fred Cawley, sent his manuscript treatise on baptism to Edinburgh University. Evans was universally regarded as a great Principal who could combine real humility with practical good sense. Students found it easy to discuss personal problems with him, and he and his wife showed many of them great personal kindness.

The College ran on a shoe-string under these devoted staff. Towards the end of their period, Taviner and Gaussen were regarded as rather old and fuddy-duddy by many of the students, but they preserved the Spurgeonic tradition, and under Evans' leadership brought fresh air and diversity to college life.

Dr Evans' lectures were not only fortified by wide and deep learning; they were also charged with spiritual purpose. In particular he set out the highest vision of the calling of pastors and shepherds of souls.

Deeply loyal to the fundamentals of the faith, to the Spurgeon tradition and to the Baptist Union, Evans was generous in spirit towards other churches. He was proud to be a Baptist, and no student could come under his influence for long without knowing that the primary duty of a Baptist minister is to build up the Kingdom of God. Nothing gave him greater pain than when a man he had trained defected from that branch of the Church that brought him into the ministry. He was a 'Father in God', not by reason of any grace bestowed by priestly hands but because of the paternal interest he always had in the training and subsequent ministry of students.

No doubt Dr Evans, like Oliver Cromwell, had a few warts but they were not remembered. People felt, as Leyton Richards felt about his own College Principal, Dr Fairbairn, 'To know the Doctor was such a bracing experience; he met you, not on your own level, but on his, and in trying to climb to that height, you breathed the tonic air in which he throve and fought.'[14]

In 1938 there was a double change of staff. Fred Cawley came to teach Old Testament, and Ron Ward came as tutor in Classical Studies. Both increased the theological breadth, spirituality and academic repute of the College. Personal factors meant that in 1950, when Evans retired, Ward was not appointed Principal as Evans wished. The job went instead to Cawley, who was ill at ease with administrative matters although a spiritually enriched man.

Frederick Cawley was born in Exmouth in 1884. At the age of fourteen he was baptised in Newton Abbot Baptist Church. He worked as a librarian prior to his acceptance by Spurgeon's College for theological training. Leaving college in 1912 he spent ten years with the Baptist Missionary Society at Bihar, India. During that time he met and married Mary Gold Coutts, a missionary teacher. In 1922 they went to the pastorate at St John's, Port of Spain, Trinidad. Four years later he accepted an invitation to Falkirk Baptist Church, Stirlingshire, where he served for nine years, applying himself to extensive reading and disciplined study. While in Falkirk he graduated in Arts and Divinity at London University, and was awarded a Doctorate in Philosophy by Edinburgh University for a thesis later published as The Transcendence of Jesus Christ. This was a study of the Person of Christ with special reference to the Gospel according to St John. In the foreword Dr H.R. Mackintosh wrote, 'Dr Cawley has earned our thanks by the insight, the reverence, and the tireless love of spiritual truth with which he has done his work.' He was called to the pastorate at Denmark Place, Camberwell in 1935. Three years later he was appointed tutor in Old Testament Studies at Spurgeon's College. He made an important and valuable contribution to the College's development during the post-war years. He was elected to the Senate of London University in 1951. From 1940 until 1946 he served as pastor of the Baptist Tabernacle, Maple Road, Penge. He and Mrs Cawley retired to Edinburgh in 1955, where his preaching ministry continued until Mrs Cawley's ill-health kept him at home to care for her. After her death in 1973 he went to reside at 'The Tor,' the Edinburgh Baptist Home for the elderly where his pastoral ministry was still welcome and where he received loving care. A keen member of Bristo Baptist Church, Edinburgh, he greatly encouraged his ministerial brethren. He died in the Royal Victoria Hospital, Edinburgh on 12 June 1978. He won deep affection and respect from those whom he served as pastor and as teacher and is remembered for his pastoral gifts, his evangelistic zeal, his missionary vision and for the spiritual quality of his very character and commitment.[15] His infectious faith in a contemporary Christ brought life into every situation.[16]

Because of his administrative gifts and experience Eric Worstead virtually became the Vice-Principal. A graduate in Arts and Divinity with First-class Honours at the University of London, he entered the College as a student in 1935. From 1939 he held pastorates at Burnham-on-Crouch and Sydenham, and in 1946 he returned to the College as a tutor of New Testament.[17]

Fig. 4.8 Principal Frederick Cawley, BA, BD, PhD (1950–1955).

The fifties were not a happy era for the College. The Principal emphasised the fine fellowship they all had enjoyed as staff, in spite of rumours of friction underlying the resignation of Dr Ward. He regretted the unwelcome severance. A resolution was drawn up as follows:

> The Council have received with much regret Dr Ward's resignation of his office as tutor consequent on his receiving an academic post. His feeling that his work for the College is done is not shared by the Council. They assure him that his service has been greatly valued, and they would be very glad if it were possible to retain his services. They trust that Dr Ward may reconsider his decision, but if this is impossible they must sorrowfully accept his resignation. They assure him of their warm good wishes for his

future, and hope that God's rich blessing may ever be with Dr and Mrs Ward and their sons.[18]

Dr Ward left partly because he was being overlooked for senior appointments and partly because he was moving in the direction of the Church of England.

The secretaryship for many of these years was in the hands of G.W. Harte. His first pastorate was at Tewkesbury (1909-1912), followed by a creative ministry at Albany Road, Cardiff (1912-1921), with a spell as a Chaplain to the Forces (1915-1920). His Army work, as for so many ministers, changed completely his conception of the ministry. From Cardiff he was called to the pastorate at Tyndale, Bristol (1921-1931), where he met T.R. Glover, for ever afterwards a deep moulding influence upon his life. His last pastorate was Elm Road, Beckenham (1931-1947). There, as elsewhere, he gathered young people about him, and influenced many for life. From 1937-1947 he also served as College Secretary part-time, and then as full-time Secretary. Perhaps, he never saw the ministry so clearly as when he was outside it, as College Secretary. He worked as BMS advocate, and chairman of committees. He advocated contact clubs as a means of reaching men.

College funds were overhauled, and more subscribers were sought and won. *The College Record* and the *Annual Report*, largely planned and carried through by Harte, became of great service. Only toward the close of his secretaryship was he also appointed warden, since that had normally been part of the Principal's responsibility. Yet from his first year in College Harte loved the men and sought to help anyone who wanted it. Continually men saw him in his office and were encouraged in their ministry.

'Billy' Harte was a man of moods, as many gifted men are, yet always loyal to his friends. Where his heart moved him he was strongly generous. He was impulsive, yet tenacious. His fertile mind drew up many schemes which only saw the light of day to die; yet others proved of abiding worth. His care for the College ran deep.[19]

Upon his death the Rev. G.W. Rusling assumed the secretaryship helped by a clerical assistant.

The removal of the College office to South Norwood Hill in 1939 completed the break with the Tabernacle. The arrival of George Beasley-Murray on the staff in 1950 accelerated the academic progress of the College. A student wrote of him:

> 'His academic attainments are known to all and we have valued them greatly. But what has made a greater impact upon us is the vitality of his personality. He exemplifies integrity, graciousness, immense energy, intense application and, transcending these, a deep devotion to Christ. The lectures he gives are always clear and interesting. He more than communicates knowledge; he communicates enthusiasm, and that is a hard thing to do in lectures. In translating the Greek text he has often delighted us with illuminating paraphrases in the modern idiom. Indeed, one of our number was moved to suggest that he should translate a "Testament for Teddy Boys". When he has led us in our devotional sessions, the experience has been rich. His handling of Scripture has always left us feeling that this is how exposition should be done. In sermon class criticism, his incisive and contructive comments have been eagerly received. Here, too, was given free reign that sense of humour, and that noiseless laughter.
>
> For you to understand why it is that we hold Dr Beasley-Murray in such affection and esteem you would have to see him as we have seen him. Talking, for instance, of energy and applica-

tion is one thing, but to see him at work is another. Whether he is preaching, lecturing, piano playing, lawn mowing, or trying to coax choir sounds from 40 raucous voices—absolutely all of his powers are hurled into the effort.[20]

His students sometimes confronted him with questions and problems which he might have preferred to avoid and at times he knew he had to risk misunderstanding. But he was determined to be loyal to the truth at all costs.[21]

Curriculum

Between 1920 and 1950 the academic repute of the College undoubtedly grew. Walter Harris was the first student to gain a Master of Theology, and even in the 1920s Vellam Pitts indicated that he was searching for a theology he did not really find in the College. Although many men were content with the College course, those whose gifts were more academic had to rely on notes from Wolsey Hall Correspondence College if they wanted to achieve a university degree whilst in college, Many could not manage this alongside their regular work, which also had to be taught, examined and certified for ministerial recognition, so many of the students of this era took their first degree when in the pastorate. It was not until the 1940s that the College's link with the London University took hold and then developed quite rapidly. In the 1920s higher criticism was avoided. Students learnt that Mark's Gospel was probably the earliest of the four, but that was about as far as New Testament criticism was carried. The name of Strauss, the liberal German was mentioned, but like an ice pond warning—'danger, keep off'. The general curriculum included Classical and New Testmaent Greek, Latin,

Hebrew, Philosophy, Psychology, Ethics, Logic, Church History, Ancient History, Critical Introduction to the Bible, Theology, Homiletics, Pastoral Theology, English Language and Literature, Biblical Background, and Elocution. Many former students mention the value of elocution, although at the time in college it was regarded as something of a joke. There was too much in the timetable, preventing a mastery of any individual subject.[22]

The curriculum was amplified by Sunday preaching in all four years, student pastorates for third year men, student evangelistic missions during college vacations, a weekly sermon class, pastoral lectures by outside speakers and a weekly discussion class.[23] There was also considerable emphasis on private study, and, although there was no specific tutorial and essay system, occasional seminar classes in batches were held with tutors on specific topics. The main teaching method was lectures; lecturers used one set text book for which to illuminate a subject. This meant that the students' minds were filled with information, but they were not given a breadth of opinion or necessarily taught to think for themselves. Study techniques and implicit instruction about devotional life were missing from the curriculum, as was any guidance for future ministers' wives. After the Second World War there was a large influx of married men and Mrs Worstead held some classes for the wives on the role of a minister's wife.

Many students acquired a smattering of languages, just sufficient to read the Scriptures and use commentaries. Everyone was taught in the same classes and encouraged to develop at their own rate. Only the very able students had an adjusted programme to enable them to take degrees. There

TIME TABLE, 1927

		Dr McCaig	Mr Gaussen	Mr P.W. Evans
Tues.	9-10	Theological Lecture (all men)		
	10-11	Senior Greek Test	Junior Latin	Middle Greek
	11-12	Senior Homiletics	Middle Latin	Junior Greek
	12-1	SERMON CLASS		
	1-2	LUNCHEON		
	2-3		Junior English Literature	Middle Church History
Wed.	9-10	Middle and Junior Theological Lecture	Senior Ethics	
	10-11	Senior Theology	Junior Logic	Middle Hebrew
	11-12	Junior New Testament Introduction	Middle Latin	Senior Greek
	12-1	Middle Greek Test	Senior Greek Test	Junior English
	1-2	LUNCHEON		
	2-3			Senior Hebrew
	8.30-9.30 pm	Elocution (Middle & Junior)		
Thurs.	9-10	Senior and Junior Church History	Middle Logic or Psychology	
	10-11	Senior Hebrew	Middle Greek Testament	Junior English or Bible study
	11-12	Middle Homiletics	Senior History Philosophy	Junior Greek
	12-1	DISCUSSION		
	1-2	LUNCHEON		
	2-3	Junior Theology	Senior Latin	Middle Greek
	5.15-6.15 pm		Science Lecture (Middle & Junior)	
Fri.	10-11	Warden's Bible Study	Junior Church History	
	11-12	Middle Pastoral Theology	Junior Greek or Roman History	

CURRICULUM FOR 1930—31

The Principal   Prof. Gaussen, MA., LL.B   Prof. Taviner, BA.   The Warden

Second, Third and Fourth Years:
Theology (The Holy Spirit).

	Old Testament Introd.
Fourth Year:	Greek Testament (Hebrew) and Contents.
The Work of Christ	Latin (Cicero).
	Hebrew (parts of Genesis and Joshua)

Third & Fourth Years:
Greek Testament (Matt) History of Philosophy   Greek (Anabasis I. Comparative Religion Ethics. Psychology and Plato's Apology. Philosophical Introduction.)

Third Year:		
Greek Test. Syntax	Latin Prose and Vergil	Hebrew Grammar
New Testament Introduction Text & Canon		(Davidson)
		Church History

Second Year:		
Homiletics & Pastoral Theology	Latin Grammar & Caesar	Hebrew Grammar (Davidson)
Greek Testament (Mk)	Greek Testament (Jn)	Greek Grammar (Initia Graeca)
Theology ('The Christian Religion in its Doctrinal Expression', by Dr E.Y. Mullins).	Psychology Logic	Church History

First Year:		Jewish History from the Exile to the Advent.
Theology (Mullins)	Latin Grammar	Greek Grammar
Early Church History	(Initia Graeca) Old Testament and New Testament Study.	
Logic	English Grammar	
	English Literature	
	Greek and Roman History	

First and Second Year men study Elocution under Mr G. Bower Codling and all Students attend the Weekly Sermon Class was no outside inspection agency during this period, and no specific denominational requirements. Special lecturers were sometimes invited to act as visiting speakers on practical and pastoral topics, although later theological topics were included. One series resulted in the publication of R.E. Clements *Old Testament Theology*.

Hebrew was obligatory, with rare exceptions. To encourage eager study, it was pointed out that this was the language our Lord knew at first hand and deeply loved. It was further suggested, as inducement, that the preacher who did not know the original tongues was often at the mercy of a biased commentator, if he could not test for himself whether an interpretation of a given passage was true and adequate exegesis. History was studied factually and spiritually. In this field, use was made of the best literature available, liberal and conservative. In the main, the ablest text books were not conservative, but liberal and semi-liberal. These books were carefully studied, and their arguments weighed academically. 'In short, our considered policy through lecture and seminar work, with the aid of the best authorities at our disposal, is to lead or guide our men to reach authoritative conviction as it bears on God, man, and destiny.'[24]

When it came to theology, Spurgeon's College endeavoured to combine two methods, which may be compared to the telescope and the microscope. At the beginning of his course it was felt that the future minister needed to survey as far as possible the whole of Christian truth, in order to grasp its inter-relatedness, or its organic nature. Four central themes of faith were therefore treated in detail, each receiving a year's study. These topics were Man, Sin and Grace; the Person of Christ; the Work of Christ; the Holy Spirit and the

Godhead. Considerable time was given to the biblical teaching, then the historical development of thought on the doctrine, and finally its setting in relation to the modern mind.

Practical application of these theological studies came out in the Sermon Classes, when the day's preacher was judged not only for the expression and delivery of his message but also for its doctrinal content and correctness. Furthermore, the practical counsel given in Pastoral Theology called again and again for consideration of the theological principles involved.[25]

No one specifically mentions the after-care of students. The only references in memories from former students were that members of their batch had retained contact. Evidently no after-care was attempted by the College officially, although the College Conference met annually and there were regular communications with students. Principals, Percy Evans especially, were very willing to offer support, encouragement and advice, but presumably the initiative had to come from individuals needing it. People tend to look back upon these years with gratitude for the benefits of community training, for the knowledge that. whatever the College's acdemic deficiencies, the emphasis on preaching, evangelism, the Cross and the Word of God had given them a firm foundation for confident ministry and a rich devotional spirit.

CHAPTER 5

The Ministry
1958–1992

THREE TIMES IN the College's history the continuance of the institution was placed in doubt. The death of C.H. Spurgeon in 1892 meant the loss of a wise leader whose personality attracted prayerful interest and financial help for the College. It was suggested that perhaps the work so long identified with the Founder should be allowed to end with his life, but Principal Gracey opposed this, saying, 'The work is of God and must go on.' In 1917, war-time conditions enforced closure, and again the issue of abandoning the enterprise was raised. Principal McCaig recalled the words of his predecessor, and again it was resolved that the work, since it was of God, must go on. It continued, and grew stronger with the years. In 1939 the probability that premises would be requisitioned for war use brought the old problem back, but it soon became clear that the former answer must again be given.

The most recent thirty years of the College's history have been led by three men who brought to the Principalship different emphases in ministry. George Beasley-Murray was the teacher, Raymond Brown the pastor, and Paul Beasley-Murray the leader. These years ended with the College training more people for the ministry than at any time since 1877. The years began, however, in turmoil and sadness.

Controversy

The 1950s were characterised by a number of difficult staff relationships which climaxed in the resignation of Eric Worstead from the Principalship in 1957 and the urgent request from the Council for George Beasley-Murray to return from Ruschlikon, where he had gone two years before as New Testament Professor. During the early fifties Eric Worstead was virtually Vice-Principal and administrative assistant to the genial, spiritual, but rather disorganised Dr Cawley. Working alongside them was the most academically gifted tutor, George Beasley-Murray, who in 1952 gained his Ph.D. from London University for his thesis on *The Eschatology of Mark 13*, Geoffrey Rusling, who had come in 1951 to teach Church History and served from 1955 as College Secretary, and Stanley Dewhurst who came to teach Christian Doctrine from 1955. In that year when Dr Cawley announced his retirement, the students went home for the Easter vacation anticipating that George Beasley-Murray would be appointed Principal. A divided Council however, opted instead for the senior tutor Eric Worstead. During his principalship the College Chapel was opened and continued improvements took place in the academic life of the College. He was spiritually revolutionised by contact with the Moral Rearmament Movement, and it was his commitment and advocacy of this which prompted a question from the Reverend Geoffrey King in the College Council in 1957, asking whether it was appropriate for the Principal of

Fig. 5.1
Principal Eric H. Worstead, BA, BD, MTh (1956–1958).

Spurgeon's College to be so committed to one particular Christian movement. A series of meetings, letters and conversations eventually resulted in Eric Worstead failing to give the desired reassurance so the College Council asked for his resignation. He left the College almost immediately and joined the Church of England, teaching at home and overseas and helping in a priestly role during his retirement at Crowborough.[1]

In 1959 Geoffrey King seconded a motion to invite Eric Worstead back onto the College Council, but the motion was never put and he did not visit the College again until 1983. From the beginning of his principalship some of the Council were against him, and his position was made more difficult by George Beasley-Murray's departure in 1955 to teach at Ruschlikon. The Reverend Frank Fitzsimmonds was brought into the faculty to teach the New Testament. In the wake of the controversy, the Council unanimously decided to consider only one candidate for the principalship, George Beasley-Murray. A number of difficulties then arose. First, it was necessary to enter into generous financial provision for the Beasley-Murray family so that he could return from Switzerland to take up the post in the summer of 1958. That inevitably created some jealousy and rivalry within the faculty who had had to carry on for a year without a Principal and were now to be led by a man receiving significantly more financial reward than they did. It was particularly difficult for Geoffrey Rusling who had spent the year as Acting Principal. There was clearly some division in the Faculty about the steps being taken. It was necessary to make some adjustment to Frank Fitzsimmonds' teaching, letting him concentrate on biblical languages, so that George Beasley-Murray could teach New

Testament Exegesis. At the time Frank Fitzsimmonds considered the possibility of returning to the pastorate, but the College was eager to hold on to his fine services, and in the end this proved a great blessing, because, as a language specialist in both Hebrew and Greek, he taught them with diligence and fruitfulness for many years. George Beasley-Murray was able to concentrate on biblical exegesis and pastoral training.

Fig. 5.2 Principal George R. Beasley-Murray, MA, PhD, DD (1958–1973).

The early years of the new principalship were clouded with difficulty, but the 1960s saw the College develop in its academic reputation and evangelistic zeal. The College at this time was predominantly a community of single men in their early twenties, and college sport, humour, and the various college societies continued to provide opportunities for students to develop outside the classroom, while the chapel helped to give fresh emphasis to the devotional life of students.

As a Principal, George Beasley-Murray encouraged by precept and example.[2] He was patient enough with those whose academic potential was limited but whose preaching and pastoral gifts were evident. He had an astonishing capacity for work. His own commitment to study and his concentration upon it could sometimes give the impression of aloofness, but once pastoral needs were drawn to his attention his concern for others was deep. His family lived on site so he also acted as warden. There were frequent visitors to the College. Each week the Principal prayed for former students by name and former students were regularly welcomed back for a Post-Collegiate Conference after eighteen months in the pastorate, when their concerns could be voiced and problems shared.

Dr Beasley-Murray wished to encourage students to present the gospel in fresh and untried ways. He did this through music, College missions and personal preaching. He developed relationships with other theological colleges, implementing the arrangements whereby six students interchanged for a week with a similar number from the Anglican College in Lincoln. He encouraged the acceptance of the first female student at Spurgeon's College in 1961, and overseas students, especially from Russia, became a regular part of the Spurgeon's community. In 1964 a new block was built consisting of a large lecture hall, nineteen study bedrooms and a spacious recreation room.

Additions were made to the staff: Rex Mason came to teach Old Testament in 1965, Lewis Drummond became the first Tutor in Evangelism and Pastoral Instruction, and in 1971 Raymond Brown was appointed to teach Church History. New interviewing structures for prospective students were introduced, probing more carefully their character and call. New technology was introduced: students' preaching in the Sermon Class was recorded on video tape. Links with America were fostered through a link with First Baptist Church, Dallas, Texas, whereby a leaving student could go for a year's internship to that large and thriving church. Staff colleagues valued the Principal's friendship and responded to his leadership; with equal warmth students responded to his scholarship

THE MINISTRY: 1958–1992

Fig. 5.3 Principal, staff and students (1965).

and his humanity. In 1973, however, he accepted an invitation to go to the United States in an attempt to devote more time to scholarly study.

The vacancy was filled by the appointment of Raymond Brown, a distinguished former student of the College, and, in his capable hands and with the co-operation of able colleagues, the proposed link with the Council for National Academic Awards, which had been George Beasley-Murray's last major enterprise, was completed and consolidated.

The 1970s ushered in an era of remarkable change, dominated by the catalyst of the CNAA.

The CNAA

From the 1930s until the mid-1970s students of Spurgeon's College were enrolled for the external BD of the University of London. In 1970, partly because of uncertainty over the future of the external BD degree and partly out of a desire to find an academic course more suited to the College's distinctive requirements, the College began negotiations with the Council for National Academic Awards regarding the appropriateness of the College as an environment for the conduct of courses leading to the award of one of the Council's degrees. In October 1972 the College submitted a formal application for validation of full-time BA and BA (Hons) degree courses in Theology. Following visits to the College by the Theological and Religious Studies Board in May 1973 and by the Officers of the CNAA in March 1974, approval was given for the full-time BA course for a period of five years from September 1974. In 1975 CNAA approval was granted for a part-time version of the course.

In November 1978 the College submitted its application for renewal of approval for the full-time and part-time BA and BA (Hons) courses. This was followed in January 1979 by a statement submitted to CNAA in preparation for the quinquennial review. The Review Checklist encourages institutions to summarise their achievements over the previous five years. These years had witnessed a steady rise in academic standards. An increase in the range of teaching and the size of the administrative and academic staff, many improvements to the premises and teaching amenities of the College, growth towards a more fully integrated course, the inauguration and development of the additional courses, the widening of the College's horizons through contact with both individuals and institutions from a variety of disciplines, and recent improvement in financial resources. The new arrangements had made the College's degree more vocationally orientated. Examination results had been very gratifying, particularly in enabling some students to obtain a degree who would not have had the minimum entrance requirements to take the London BD formerly.

Fig. 5.4 Principal Raymond Brown, MA, BD, MTh, PhD (1973–1986).

In 1976 Michael Nicholls was appointed to the staff to develop a separate course leading to the Cambridge Diploma in Religious Studies. Part-time courses, involving day-release attendance for both degree and diploma studies, were successfully introduced. A new postgraduate Pastoral Studies

Course was set up, after a pilot year, giving fourth year students insights into the work of the minister in the contemporary world and widening the total educational experience. The teaching staff had been increased from five to eight, with the appointment of Martin Selman to teach Old Testament, Bruce Milne to teach Christian Doctrine, Stanley Dewhurst as part-time Librarian following his years of full-time service, Brian Stanley as Academic Registrar and Peter Manson to teach pastoral studies. Staff were encouraged to take advantage of sabbatical leave facilities, undertake academic research and participate in writing projects. Consistent improvements were made to the library, and in 1985 Judy Powles was appointed the College's first trained Librarian. A Board of Studies involving external academics had been set up to offer a different perspective and informed criticism of the College's life and courses. Adequate financial resources had met the needs of the new courses and full-time student enrolment had risen from fifty-three to seventy-five. Student involvement in the affairs of the College had also been developed, with three representatives as full members of the College's governing Council.

On 23 February 1979 a CNAA delegation visited the College for a joint course and institutional review. As a result of the visit, the Theological and Religious Studies Board agreed to re-approve the BA/BA (Hons) full-time and part-time courses for five years from September 1979, subject to three conditions, which the College met by submitting revised proposals in December 1979. With regard to the institutional review, the visiting party recommended to Council that the College should be approved as an acceptable environment for the Council's awards for a further period of five years from

September 1979. Four specific recommendations were attached to the renewal of approval, which can be summarised as follows:

i) that the College should make further progress towards establishing an open academic community;
ii) that the College should review the overall timetable and staff commitment in order to facilitate staff engagement in research and scholarly activities;
iii) that the Board of Studies should undertake an evaluation of the future role of the College and its potential avenues of development;
iv) that the College should give serious consideration to various recommendations on the Library.

The central criticism made by Council's 1984 visiting party and report related to the inadequacy of the College's management and committee structures, particularly in relation to course monitoring and evaluation procedures. They were also concerned about the apparent lack of a clear policy for resource planning and allocation. This line of criticism was discussed at some length both in the Academic Board and in meetings of the College Officers and Executive Committee. The College conceded the cogency and justice of the criticism.

Before the commencement of the CNAA BA course in 1974, academic policy and decision-making at Spurgeon's was in the hands of the small team of full-time staff, meeting weekly in the staff meeting. There was no Academic Board of any kind. Overall responsibility was exercised by the College's governing body, the College Council, but this was composed largely of serving Baptist ministers and laymen whose expertise was not primarily in matters of academic policy or course content. Financial policy and resource allocation were the personal prerogative of the laymen who served the College in a voluntary capacity as successive Treasurers.

Since the early 1970s developments had combined to render this mode of management increasingly inadequate. The College had expanded in terms of numbers of staff, students and range of courses. CNAA validation had raised the academic standards of the College and dictated corresponding improvements in the quality of its library resources. The annual budget had increased enormously at the same time as income from Local Education Authority Grants for students had become more precarious. In response to these changes the College set up a series of new committees: a Board of Studies to run the CNAA courses, a Candidate's Selection Committee to process the greater numbers of applicants for ministerial training and, a Revenue and Resources Committee to maximise the College's voluntary income.

Whilst all these innovations were necessary and proved their value, the institutional development of the College was nevertheless of an *ad hoc* character. Two crucial areas of management appeared in retrospect to have been in some measure neglected. The first was overall academic policy. The Board of Studies was given largely formal responsibilities relating to the CNAA courses, had nothing to do with the Cambridge Diploma or Diploma in Pastoral Studies courses, and in practice took few initiatives in policy development. The Pastoral Studies Diploma remained as before in the hands of the staff meeting, which involved only full-time staff.

The second area of weakness was that of corporate responsibility for resource allocation: the Revenue and Resources Committee was concerned merely with the College's income—expenditure continued to be left in large measure to the personal control of the College Treasurer. Major decisions on expenditure were taken by the College Council or Executive Committee, but the Board of Studies had very little influence in determining the allocation of resources. Academic planning and resource allocation were, in fact, seen as separate aspects of College management with limited communication between the bodies responsible for the two areas.

Major stuctural changes take time to implement but eventually a new, more developed committee emerged.

Courses

In the College Council, in the early 1960s, reference was made to concern about academic life:

> Studies of the students have been a matter of concern to the teaching staff. The examination results in June 1961 were very bad. Four men failed Final BD, four failed Inter BD (three were in their first year). Three men who had been referred in one subject in Inter BD a year earlier gained their Inter BD by various ways—two by taking a GCE 'A' Level in January last and one by taking Hebrew instead of the subject earlier failed. Thirteen attempted the new preliminary BD examination: eight passed and five failed (of these latter three were in the first year). In the GCE Advanced Level examinations three gained one 'A' Level and one 'O' Level passes.

COLLEGE STRUCTURE

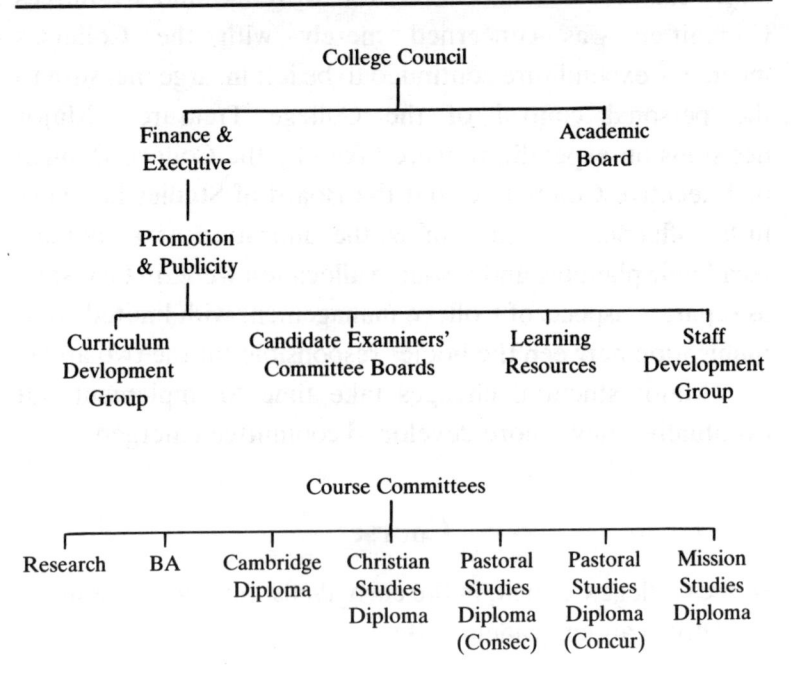

```
                        College Council
                              |
        ┌─────────────────────┴─────────────────┐
     Finance &                              Academic
     Executive                               Board
        |
    Promotion
    & Publicity
        |
  ┌─────────────┬──────────────────┬──────────────┬──────────────┐
  Curriculum   Candidate Examiners'    Learning      Staff
  Devlopment   Committee  Boards       Resources     Development
  Group                                              Group

                      Course Committees
                              |
  ┌────────┬────────┬──────────┬──────────┬──────────┬──────────┐
 Research  BA   Cambridge  Christian   Pastoral   Pastoral   Mission
              Diploma     Studies    Studies    Studies    Studies
                          Diploma    Diploma    Diploma    Diploma
                                     (Consec)   (Concur)
```

Reasons for these failures were given and the students were warned that greater effort must be made, but the sober fact needed to be faced by the executive committee and council: there were limitations on what the teaching staff could achieve with some students. The staff agreed that students must not be permitted to attempt qualifications which were beyond their abilities, even if it meant foregoing a grant.

As well as the influence of the CNAA on college management and the degree course, the 1970s and 1980s saw a remarkably diverse development of college courses to take account of changing patterns in the churches and in the students coming forward. From being a community of single men, the College developed into a training ground for men and women, three-quarters of whom were married and over half of whom had families. The average age of the students rose from twenty-two to thirty-five. New accommodation had to be provided in the old faculty house, where Frank Fitzsimmonds lived until 1983, and in the house in South Norwood kindly donated by the Humphrey family. These houses were converted into a total of nine married flatlets. Further rooms were converted within the College to offer accommodation for up to seventeen couples and families. Alternative residences were found in vacant manses and other rented properties around south London. Influenced by both the ecumenical and the charismatic movements, the concept of ministers changed. Churches wanted men and women of experience who were willing to work in teams, who specialised in certain areas and enabled others to develop their gifts alongside them. This required a new emphasis on diversity, personality, self-awareness and personal relationships. To meet this diverse situation the College developed three types of course.

1. College-based courses where students attended the College for five days a week and undertook practical experience at weekends. In their first year the practical experience consisted of a student assistantship, in the second year a student pastorate, and in the third and fourth years itinerant preaching or sabbatical cover.
2. A Church-based course during which a student would attend the College on one or two days a week and would spend four or five days engaged in church

experience. Church experience was considered part of training and was carefully monitored and evaluated so that the student was learning on the job. This course was particularly relevant for those who had entered the Baptist ministry through a calling to local churches without ever having attended a Baptist college.
3. The Mission-based course was similar to the church-based model but was particularly appropriate for the pastor/evangelist who was to be a mission leader rather than a conventional pastor/teacher. A new Diploma in Mission Studies was developed to meet this particular need.

Recognising that students' ability was varied, a separate Spurgeon's College Diploma course was run from 1976 based on the Cambridge Diploma in Religious Studies. This was eventually taught through evening classes, day-release courses, and distance learning, as well as lectures and seminars for the full-time College-based students. An alternative College Diploma/Certificate in Christian Studies was validated by the College in 1989 for those for whom continual assessment works better than examination. This became particularly popular with the student wives. A full series of evening classes was run from 1972 onwards, when up to two hundred attended the College on Mondays and Tuesdays for academic, theological, biblical and pastoral instruction. A series of Summer Schools, block weeks and Leadership Weekends also provided a forum for lay training. The College was thus able to provide for virtually anyone who wanted to train for the Baptist ministry whatever their circumstances, and to provide for the growing number of pastoral assistants, elders, deacons, administrators, counsellors, housegroup leaders and so on, some appropriate training that would build on their skills and develop their biblical awareness and theological understanding.

In the last few months of 1976, one wing of the main college building was given a new look, and partly opened in November as the Pastoral Studies Centre. There, three rooms came into full use in October 1977. The Pastoral Studies Diploma was to be awarded after the satisfactory completion of projects, seminars, and lectures in the final year at College. Seven areas were covered:

1. Psychology and Pastoral Work—practical training with special reference to pastoral counselling in such areas as adolescence, marriage, retirement, grief.
2. Sociology and Pastoral Work—for example, the community, the family, racial integration, not only in terms of pastoral care and ministry, but also evangelism.
3. Communication of the Gospel—preaching, the use of the media, audio-visual aids.
4. Theology and History of Mission—to provide a clear background to our role and work.
5. Church Administration—pattern of church life, church offices, meetings, the church and legal matters.
6. Christian Education—examining the Church's training of its people at all stages; the day school and Christian education; the minister in school.

7. Christian Worship—its nature and expression in principle and in practice.

Staff

The staff complement doubled in this period. Raymond Brown's Principalship, from 1973 to 1986, combined scholarship, teaching gifts and deep personal spiritual commitment which enriched the life of the College. He commanded respect and affection and his preaching gifts were widely acknowledged, both in this country and overseas. His pastoral care was particularly significant. His scholarship was evident in his academic exposition and devotional works which have extended his own personal ministry to a very wide constituency. His own academic achievements, particularly the rare award of a Cambridge BD, underlined his deep conviction to do and be the best for Christ's sake. With his wife Christine, a warm welcome was given to their home, so people in genuine need were ministered to. His own home became a centre for evangelistic outreach and he faithfully encouraged students to become preachers of the Word and evangelistically hearted pastors. Dr Brown was joined by a gifted and united staff.

After working in insurance in the City of London, John Maile studied at Spurgeon's College between 1976 and 1971, gaining a first-class honours degree in Theology. Three years' pastoral ministry at Old Lodge Lane Baptist Church, Purley, was followed by a return to the College in 1974, first as a research fellow and then as Tutor in New Testament. A fast-talking lecturer, informed conversationalist and popular preacher, he was an original thinker. His contributions to the College Sermon Class were incisive and helpful. He enriched his biblical lectures with comprehensive notes which have been widely used. Quiet, thoughtful, calm and relaxed, he always spoke with authority and gave the teaching of New Testament a high and acceptable profile in College life.

Peter Manson came in 1975 from the church at Woolwich to be responsible for teaching the practical courses and the presiding genius over the unique fourth-year Course in Pastoral Studies. He became well-known, especially in South Wales, and much appreciated as a preacher of great energy, enthusiasm and firm biblical conviction. His evening class in Pastoral Care and Counselling was for many years consistently the most popular of the College's evening programme.

As an Old Testament lecturer between 1965 and 1974, Rex Mason was the antithesis of the popular notion of an Old Testament pundit—restless, ebullient, lively, and leading the laughter in any social group, and unaffectedly enjoying other people's jokes as well as his own. He possessed the gift of winning and holding interest. The Old Testament was seen to be alive as he skilfully handled its problems and showed its relevance for the preacher. His achievements in Old Testament scholarship, have been marked particularly by the award of a London Ph.D. and by his inclusion in a panel of Old Testament translators, and he also became competent in a new field of study, Christian Ethics. His versatility was shown when he was able to draw on an earlier qualification in English to teach a new degree subject in Religion and Literature.

When Rex Mason moved to Regent's Park College, Oxford, he was followed by the more conservative and Christocentric Martin Selman, who enabled the College to offer undergraduate courses not only in Hebrew but in Aramaic and Akkadian as well. Eminently well-qualified, with a first-class honours degree from University of Wales followed by a Ph.D. and practical archaeological experience, he enriched every facet of College life and continued his activity in research and biblical translation.

In 1973 Bruce Milne came to the College, first to teach Evangelism and Pastoral Studies and then to design and teach the new course in Theology. With an alert mind and immense capacity for hard work, he skilfully blended scholarship and spirituality. He was able critically to examine a wealth of theological ideas, explain the teaching of others with fairness and evaluate their importance and relevance for contemporary living. A gifted expository preacher, popular in Christian Union meetings at various universities, he was also a skilled author.

From 1979 onwards, Brian Stanley oversaw the development of the College library and handled links with the CNAA. His mental powers, attention to detail, administrative skill and ability to communicate accurately and carefully, all contributed to the College's good standing with the Council for National Academic Awards. A gifted and well-qualified historian, especially in the field of modern missions, Dr Stanley is a gifted preacher and author, not least of the Bicentenary history of the Baptist Missionary Society.

It was an adventurous decision of the College Council in 1984 to invite Bob and Shirley Thompson to come from their New Zealand Baptist College for three years to follow Bruce Milne in the teaching of theology. It is never easy for someone to come from a different culture and ecclesiastical scene, but Bob worked hard to produce copious theological material and to assist the students in their work. He brought his pastoral experience to College life, and as an assiduous reader and voluminous writer, he broadened the perspective of staff and students alike.

During the last three years of Ray Brown's Principalship, 1983-86, three problems arose in the life of the College:

1. The Principal was considering the possibility of moving to a pastorate, so when Frank Fitzsimmonds, the Vice-Principal retired, and Bruce Milne, the prospective Vice-Principal left to take up a Canadian pastorate within six months of each other in 1983, J.J. Brown, a former College Chairman and Secretary, was appointed the Principal's Deputy. This precautionary measure meant that the leadership of the College was in the hands of Ray Brown, J.J. Brown and George Cumming, who was the College Chairman. All three were senior in years and different in outlook from the emerging generation of ministers.
2. In 1984 the College's renewal application to the CNAA met with limited success. The degree was only renewed for two years and that subject to considerable work on the contextual strand of the course. This concern dominated College life over the next eighteen months and Ray Brown felt he had to stay whilst this was implemented.
3. Although the College's pattern of church-based training was ready in 1984, it was not actually implemented until 1986 because priority had to be given to changes in the degree course structure. This meant that at a time when similar patterns were available at Northern and Regent's Park Colleges, the Spurgeon's courses seemed rather inflexible.

As a consequence of these three factors, the numbers coming into College in 1984 and 1985 were fairly small, batches of under fifteen, and the general image of the College was anti-charismatic and staid. This worried the Council, and when Dr Brown announced that he intended to leave by the summer of 1987 at the latest, but was willing to go in 1986 if a suitable appointment was made, a search was begun in earnest for the right kind of leader. An Appointments Committee was set up in 1985 by the College Council with a threefold remit: to investigate the present state of College life and the gifts of the present faculty, draw up a clear job description, and bring a nomination to the College Council. After considerable negotiation Paul Beasley-Murray was adopted by the College Council.

The new principal grew up at the College during the days when his father was principal, from 1958 to 1973. He himself was educated at Jesus College, Cambridge, and the Northern Baptist College, with further specialist study experience at Manchester University and Zurich. After receiving his Ph.D. from Manchester in 1970 he served for two years with the Baptist Missionary Society in Zaire, teaching in the Protestant Theology Faculty of the University of Kisangani. He returned to Britain in 1972 and the following year commenced his ministry at Altrincham. During his thirteen year pastorate there, the church grew and developed substantially. He wrote extensively and enjoyed an international ministry, particularly to colleges and seminaries in Europe and the Commonwealth, where he was recognised as an expert on Church Growth.

He saw his task as Principal in terms of advancing the cause of Christ and his kingdom through the fulfilment of the Great Commission—'Go to all peoples everywhere and make disciples... baptise and teach them.' He also saw the College making a constant contribution to Baptist life around the world, through the BMS and in contacts with Baptist people in Europe, both East and West. He wanted the College to be known as both evangelical and open to all that God was doing in the modern world.

The Rev. Arthur Thompson, Metropolitan Area Superintendent and chairman of the College's Principalship Appointments Committee, said the committee's brief had been to find a man 'who would take the College into the twenty-first century'. The post when advertised had stressed the need for a spiritual leader for the College. The early months of the new Principalship were a time of considerable anticipation. It was envisaged that a sum of £1,000,000 would be raised through an appeal. In reality only £100,000 was raised and early promise gave way to some disappointment. In January 1987 the College Council was plunged into crisis when the College Officers at the time resigned after a dispute over fiscal management. Gradually the controversy and its effects receded and the life of the College settled down to a period of considerable change and developement.

Colourful and controversial, Paul Beasley-Murray stamped his image upon the College as an open, adventurous person, confident in his own abilities and eager to use modern techniques to develop the public image of the College. During the late 80s and early 90s the College developed rapidly: expenditure increased, income grew, buildings developed, staff numbers increased and student numbers escalated. The leadership was robust and attracted the admiration of the wider Christian world. Sadly confidence and trust were less in evidence within the College Community and the Principalship came to a premature end in 1992.

College Ethos

Throughout the years students have developed their devotional life by participation in the life of local churches, student assistantships, student pastorates, engagement in student missions and other forms of evangelism, morning devotions, lectures commencing and ending with prayers, Sermon Class and other preaching engagements, the Prayer Partnership Scheme, batch prayer meetings, regular prayers for former students and missionaries overseas, Self-Awareness Groups, Marriage Enrichment Weekends, personal quiet times, College Hours and Whitehouse Missionary Fellowship talks. In recent years there has been an increasing awareness of spirituality in all its rich and varied traditions. That breadth and awareness is due in part to the vision that Paul Beasley-Murray brought to the College. In spite of the sad end to his Principalship, it is right to record with gratitude the obvious benefits and progress of the years between 1986 and 1992.

Fig. 5.5 Principal Paul Beasley-Murray, MA, PhD (1986–1992).

During those years the College increased its staff with

able communicators. Stuart Christine came in 1988, first to teach New Testament and then to develop the new course, in partnership with the Oasis Trust, in Church Planting and Evangelism. An Oxford and Spurgeon's graduate, he had served for ten years in Brazil in pastoral work and church planting. He and his family returned to Brazil in 1992.

Until 1986 Nigel Wright was Senior Pastor of Ansdell Baptist Church, Lytham St Annes. Well-qualified academically, gifted pastorally and enthusiastically committed to the renewal movement, Nigel has taught theology with distinction and enthusiasm. He has served as Chairperson of Mainstream and played an influential part in the renewal of denominational structures.

Debra Reid became the first female member of faculty in 1987, heading up the Diploma teaching and enriching the Old Testament department. In 1990 Bob Archer was appointed the first Tutor in Church-Based Training, following distinguished pastorates in Bournemouth, Canterbury, Worcester Park and Reading. Alastair Campbell, an Oxford graduate, came after fourteen years' pastoral experience in Northampton, first to do research and was then appointed New Testament Tutor. Colin Brown worked part-time from 1984 and was appointed a full-time Tutor in 1990. He brought to the College wide experience of the academic world, following a career in education, and taught Philosophy and Ethics with quality and stimulation. A former colleague of his, Arthur Rowe, came in 1991 to assist in the teaching of New Testament and to broaden the scope of the College teaching as the first full-time member of staff to teach World Religions.

Through the students trained at the Pastors' College and their subsequent service, the Spurgeon tradition, committed to Jesus, the Cross, the Bible, the gospel, faith, prayer and the work of the Spirit, has continued to have global influence. Of the 2,300 students trained at the College through its history, 116 have come from twenty-six different overseas countries and many have returned to those countries as their sphere of service. In the early days the greater number came from Australia and Canada, but in the twentieth century Russia, Brazil, Europe and Africa have provided more. A total of 467 former students, over a fifth, have served overseas in forty-one different countries at some point in their ministry. Again the dominant countries of service have been Australia and Canada, together with the United States, South Africa, Zaire, India and China. Twenty countries have received no more than two students, but each individual has taken back to their particular location something of the ethos, atmosphere and commitment of the College. A greater number of men served overseas in the 1870s and 80s, but during the hundred and thirty-four year history of the College only sixteen batches have failed to send at least one person overseas. Many have gone with the Baptist Missionary Society, but others simply returned to their country of origin and yet others went with independent missionary societies.

The College has sought to play its part in the wider Christian world. Initially an independent entity, the College has throughout the twentieth century played an increasing part in co-operation with other Baptist colleges in Great Britain and with the structures and officers of the Baptist Union. Sadly in recent years links with the Reformed ministry at the Metropolitan Tabernacle have become tenuous and fragile. Through formal structures like the College's Joint Consultative Committee and more informal networks of fellowship and influence, the College, with others, has been able to promote a spirit of complementarity rather than competition among Baptist colleges. Links have been fostered especially with the Irish Baptist College, All Nations Christian College, Oak Hill Theological College and with the wider academic world through the Consortium of Theological Colleges linked with the Council for National Academic Awards. Although never strong in formal ecumenical links, the College has become less and less isolated from mainstream Christian life reflected in many different traditions. Increasingly conscious also of the wider educational world through the CNAA, the College has been able to play a leading role among private institutions outside the university sector and also to contribute to a more flexible understanding of ministry within the Baptist denomination. That understanding of ministry expressed by Paul Beasley-Murray affirms:

1. All God's people are called to and gifted for 'ministry' (see 1 Cor.12:4-11; also Eph. 4:7,12). Every Christian has a part to play if the body of Christ is to function properly. In a very real sense every Christian is called to be a 'minister' ('minister' is, of course, simply the Latin word for 'servant').
2. Yet, along with the ministry of all, the Scriptures clearly point to the leadership of some (see Rom. 12:8; 1 Cor. 12:28; Eph. 4:11). At local church level such leadership may be given by elders and/or deacons. However, spearheading the leadership team will normally be the pastor, whom God has called and gifted for this particular service. The content of that leadership is exercised in particular through the preaching and teaching of God's word (Eph. 4:11; 1 Tim. 3:2; cf also Acts 6:4), through the oversight of God's people (Acts 20:28; 1 Pet. 5:2) and through the equipping of God's people for service (Eph. 4:11–

12). An evangelistic thrust will also be a mark of such ministry (2 Tim. 4:5).
3. That leadership is not restricted to men. The Scriptures teach that the Spirit gives gifts irrespective of gender (Acts 2:17–18). Although certain cultural situations have limited leadership to men (see 1 Cor. 11:3–6; 14:33–36; 1 Tim. 2:11–15), in principle there is no Scriptural reason why women should not share the leadership (thus Paul in Romans 16:1–3, 7. mentions women serving as deacons, teachers, and apostles). There can be no superiority of male over female in Christ (Gal. 3:28).
4. A call to leadership amongst God's people has various components:
   (a) The call needs to be sensed within the life of the individual. However, just as there is no stereotyped conversion experience, so too there is no fixed pattern of call. A call, for instance, need not be dramatic by nature—the experience of Isaiah in the temple is no more typical of a call than is the experience of Paul on the Damascus Road typical of conversion. Nonetheless, common to all those called of God to leadership among his people will be a sense of inward constraint (1 Cor. 9:16) and a real desire to serve the Lord in such a way (1 Tim. 3:1).
   (b) The call will be evidenced by appropriate gifts for leadership. In order to lead God's people, the prospective pastor will need to be able to communicate effectively (1 Tim. 3:2) and relate helpfully to others (1 Tim. 3:3). An ability to think, and a facility for self-awareness, are equally vital.
   (c) The call will be evidenced by character (see 1 Tim. 3:1–7). Love, humility, holiness, industry, perseverance—such characteristics are essential for Christian leadership. The test of character is fundamental to the call of God. Gifts without character are worthless. The life of a leader must be marked by spiritual authenticity discernible both within and without the church (see 1 Tim. 3:7).
   (d) The genuineness of the call must be recognised by the people of God. Such 'objective' recognition may at times

precede the 'subjective' call within the life of the individual, in the sense that on occasion people within the church may take the initiative and share their conviction that God is indeed calling a particular individual to leadership in God's church (see Acts 13:1–3). Usually, however, it is the potential candidate who submits a subjective sense of call to the scrutiny of the local church.

(e) The call needs to be further tested by the wider church. In today's Baptist context, this is first done by the local Association through its Ministerial Recognition Committee, and then through one of our Baptist Colleges which in its acceptance procedures tests the call on behalf of the Baptist Union of Great Britain.

(f) As part of the on-going testing process, the candidate will receive appropriate training, for gifts need to be developed, character needs to be moulded, the mind needs to be stretched and informed, and practical ministry skills need to be imparted. Training is not just desirable, it is necessary if competent leadership is to be exercised among God's people today.

(g) The call is only finally confirmed when the candidate receives and accepts the call from God's people to exercise pastoral leadership amongst them. It is at this stage that ordination takes place, as the wider church then gives public recognition to God's call.

And so the story continues. Called men and women continue to come to be trained for pastoral leadership in evangelical churches throughout the world. They are taught in a community of teachers, administrators, cooks, cleaners and maintenance people, all playing their part, and supported by a host of grateful people whose gifts and prayers are the backbone of the work.

Fig. 5.6 Spurgeon's College (1992).

Notes

Introduction

1. J.C. Carlile, *C.H. Spurgeon: An Interpretative Biography* (1933), p.171.
2. See 'Bampfield's Plan for an Educated Ministry' in *Transactions of the Baptist Historical Society*, 3 (1912–13), p.17. The author of this article is not named but the style is characteristic of W.T. Whitley. Davison died in 1721 and was succeeded both as pastor and tutor by Thomas Lucas. In 1737 the church in Paul's Alley, Barbican, voted certain of the books in its considerable library for the use of the academy under Lucas. W. Wilson, *History and Antiquities of Dissenting Churches and Meeting Houses in London, Westminster and Southwark* (1810) vol.2, p.231.
3. S. Gummer, 'Trosnant Academy', *Baptist Quarterly*, 9 (1938–39), an article which corrects the compressed and somewhat misleading reference to this academy in E.J. Price, 'Dissenting Academies, 1661–1820', *Baptist Quarterly*, 6 (1932–33), p.135.
4. Price *op. cit.* p.132. See also 'Sutcliff's Academy at Olney', *Baptist Quarterly*, 4 (1928–29), p.276. The author of this unsigned article is M.M. Hewitt, *Baptist Quarterly*, 6 (1932–33), p.124.
5. 'The General Baptist Academy of the Old Connexion, *Baptist Quarterly*, 3 (1926–27), pp.331–2. The note is unsigned.
6. For Bampfield, see entry in *Dictionary of National Biography*.
7. Edited by Ivimey, *History of the English Baptists*, 1811, vol.1, p.492.
8. *ibid*. p.513.
9. *ibid*. pp.534–5.
10. *Baptist Quarterly*, 4 (1928–29), p.293.
11. T.F. Valentine, Concern for the Ministry: the story of the Particular Baptist Fund, 1717–1967, Teddington, 1967.
12. One such was William Clark, minister at Unicorn Yard, Southwark, 1762–85. Ivimey says that as a scholar Clark's acquirements were considerable and 'the Particular Baptist Fund in London judged him a proper person to instruct others whose views were directed to sanctuary service', Ivimey, vol.4, p.397.
13. The first tutor was the distinguised classical scholar Thomas Llewellyn, 1720–93. Trained at Trosnant, he had already begun to train men for the ministry at Hammersmith when he was approached by the new Society. See *Baptist Quarterly*, 9 (1938–9), pp.421ff, and J.W. Ashley-Smith, *Birth of Education*.
14. G.P. Gould, *The Baptist College at Regent's Park: A Century Record*, 1910, pp.14–16.
15. W. Brook, 'John Ward, LLD., FRS., FSA., *Transactions of the Baptist Historical Society*, 4 (1914–15), p.26. Ward, for whom see *Dictionary of National Biography*, was an original trustee of the British Museum.
16. E.J. Tongue, 'Dr John Ward's Trust', *Baptist Quarterly*, 4 (1949–50), p.221.

17. B.M. Himbury, *Baptist Quarterly*, 21 (1966) No.8, p.340.
18. R.E. Cooper, *From Stepney to St Giles*, P.19.
19. John Gill quoted in B.M. Himbury, *Baptist Quarterly*, 21 (1966), No.8, p.341.
20. A. Fuller, *Address to the Students at Stepney*, 24 June 1811.
21. I. Mann, *Address to the Students of the Northern Academy*, 1829.
22. N. Moon, *Education for Ministry* (1979), p.28.
23. W. Jones, *Address to the Students at Abergavenny*, 1830.
24. *Regent's Park College Annual Report* (1885), p.43.
25. *ibid*. Historical Notice, p.5.
26. Cambridge, St Andrew's Street Church Book, 72A.
27. Soham Church Book, 9/78.
28. *Baptist Magazine*, 1820, p.21.
29. *ibid*. 1848, pp.16–18.
30. *Regent's Park College Annual Report* (1853), pp.15–16.

Chapter 1: The Governor

1. J.C. Carlile, *C.H. Spurgeon: An Interpretative Biography* (1933), p.169.
2. C.H. Spurgeon, *The New Park Street Pulpit* (1863–4), vol.1, p.268.
3. Carlile, *op.cit*. p.171.
4. C.H. Spurgeon, *The Sword and the Trowel* (1881), p.175.
5. 'Honorat in the opening years of the fifth century retired to the little island near Cannes which still bears his name, and attracted around him a number of students. The one best known to us is Patrick, the evangelizer of Ireland... Thus did Honorat and Columba in the olden days, and so did Wycliffe and Luther and Calvin in the Reformation times, train the armies of the Lord for their Mission. Schools of the prophets are a prime necessity if the power of religion is to be kept alive and propagated in the land.' C.H. Spurgeon, *Autobiography* (1890), (1899), vol.3, p.137. 'We talk of Luther and Calvin in the days of the Reformation but we must remember that these men became what they were largely through their power to stamp their image and superscription upon other men with whom they came into contact. If you went to Wurtemberg it was not only Luther that you saw but Luther's College—the men around him—the students all being formed into young Luthers under his direction. It was the same at Geneva. How much Scotland owes to the fact that Calvin could instruct John Knox! How much have other nations derived from the little republic of Switzerland on account of Calvin's having the clear common sense to perceive that one man could not hope to affect a whole nation except by multiplying himself, and spreading his views by writing them upon the fleshly tablets of the hearts of young and earnest men! The Churches seem to have forgotten this. It is nothing but sanctified common sense that leads the church for the formation of a college. The church ought to make the college the first object of its care.' G.H. Pike, *The Life and Work of Charles Haddon Spurgeon* (1892), vol.4, p.356.
6. *The Sword and the Trowel* (1884), p.307ff.
7. *The Sword and the Trowel* (1881), p.175.
8. Carlile, p.171.
9. *ibid*
10. *The Sword and the Trowel* (1887), p.206.
11. *The Sword and the Trowel* (1889), p.311.

NOTES

12. C.H. Spurgeon *Autobiography* vol.2 (1898), p.148.
13. Rogers, *Annual Report*, 1866.
14. William Williams, *Personal Reminiscences of C.H. Spurgeon* (1895), p.193.
15. C.H. Spurgeon *Autobiography* (1890), vol.2, p.149.
16. *The Sword and the Trowel* (1889), p.311.
17. Anon, *Charles Haddon Spurgeon: A Biographical Sketch And Appreciation by One Who Knew Him Well* (1903), p.139.
18. G.H. Pike (1892), vol.1, p.233.
19. W.Y. Fullerton, *The Life and Works of Charles Haddon Spurgeon: A Biography* (1903), p.232.
20. *Annual Report* 1867, p.3. A. McDougall, a student from the Metropolitan Tabernacle who went to pastor a church at Rothesay after training, bore testimony to the intellectual situation: 'My knowledge of the English language was very defective; I had heard about mathematics but did not know what the word meant. I had never declined a Latin noun and as for Greek, I did not know the letters.' *ibid.* p.39.
21. *The Sword and the Trowel* (1882), p.258.
22. E.A. Payne, *The Baptist Union: A Short History* (1959), p.71.
23. *Annual Report* 1870, p.7.
24. F.W. Harte, *Historical Tablets of the Pastors' College*, pp.10–11.
25. *The Sword and the Trowel* (1881), p.302.
26. *The New York Examiner*, 1869.
27. C.H. Spurgeon, *The New York Street Pulpit* (1863–4), p.352.
28. C.H. Spurgeon, *Autobiography* (1890), vol.2, pp.215, 283–4.
29. *Annual Report*, 1866, p.43.
30. *ibid* p.398.
31. *The Sword and the Trowel* (1887), p.509.
32. J.M. Campbell, *The Nature of the Atonement*, Sixth Edition, p.117.
33. F.D. Maurice, *Theological Essays*, Fifth Edition, p.126.
34. M. Arnold, *St Paul & Protestantism, With an Essay on Puritanism & The Church of England*, pp.162–3.
35. F.W. Farrar, *Eternal Hope*, pp.XXIII–XXIV. See also Sermon on 'Hell'— What it is Not', pp.49–89.
36. C.H. Spurgeon, *Autobiography*, vol.4, 1900, p.253.
37. H. Davies, *Worship and Theology in England* (1962), vol.4, p.333. John Kent emphasises the point too strongly when he says: 'His reaction to the effect of biblical criticism on the Baptist Ministry had been to set up a college for training pastors himself', *Holding the Fort*, 1978, pp.303–4.
38. *ibid.* p.333.
39. *ibid.* p.333.
40. C.H. Spurgeon, *Autobiography* (1890), vol.1, 1897, p.104. He found most help in Bunyan's writings; Doddridge's *The Rise and Progress of Religion in the Soul*; Baxter's *Call to the Unconverted*; Alleine's *Alarm to Sinners*; and J.A. James's *Anxious Enquirer*.
41. 'My own model, if I have such a thing, in due subordination to my Lord, is George Whitefield.' C.H. Spurgeon, *Autobiography* (1890), vol.2, p.66.
42. *Annual Report*, 1871, p.5.
43. J.C. Carlile (1933), p.289. *C.H. Spurgeon: An Interpretative Biography*.
44. Spurgeon's library contained over 12,000 volumes, of which approximately 1,000

were printed before 1700. The oldest volume is dated 1525. The bulk of the collection was purchased by the trustees of William Jewell College in 1905 for $3,500 and is now located at William Jewell College, Liberty, Missouri.
45. *Annual Report*, 1866, p.14.
46. *The Sword and the Trowel* (1871), p.227.
47. *The Sword and the Trowel* (1881), p.309.
48. *The Sword and the Trowel* (1887), pp.122–6 and 166–172. In these 'Downgrade' articles the decline of eighteenth century Nonconformity is attributed largely to the theological colleges.
49. *Annual Report*, 1881, p.1.
50. C.H. Spurgeon, *Autobiography* (1890), vol.2, pp.250–1.
51. *The Sword and the Trowel* (1883), pp.262–3.
52. C.H. Spurgeon, *Lectures to My Students*, 1877, p.5.
53. John Clifford, *The English Baptists* (1881), pp.26–7.
54. Cited by C.W. Johnson, *Encounter in London* (1985), p.47.
55. H. Thielicke, *Encounter with Spurgeon*, p.28.
56. H. Davies, *Worship and Theology in England* (1962), IVP, p.355.
57. E.A. Payne, *The Free Church Tradition in the Life of England*, p.109. A.C. Underwood, *A History of the English Baptists* (1947), p.219.
58. Spurgeon's early education was in the hands of his grandfather. Between the ages of ten and twelve he spent some months at two Home schools run by Mrs Cook and Mr Lewis. At the age of fourteen he spent a year at All Saints Agricultural College, Maidstone.
59. Payne, *op.cit.* p.109.
60. C.H. Spurgeon, *Autobiography* (1890), vol.3, p.137.
61. *ibid.* vol.2, p.149.
62. Spurgeon, *Lectures*, p.2 of Second Series.
63. *Metropolitan Tabernacle Pulpit*, 31, p.291.
64. Spurgeon, *Lectures*, p.184, Second Series.
65. *Metropolitan Tabernacle Pulpit*, 34, p.187.

Chapter 2: The Institution

1. *1.Congregational Year Book* (1892), p.195.
2. Dr Archibald McCaig, BA, LLB, *Presidential Address* to *the Conference of Spurgeon's College*, April 13 1926, p.3.
3. *The Baptist Handbook* (1862), p.28.
4. McCaig, *op.cit.* p.3.
5. *Spurgeon's College Annual Report* (1892), p.383.
6. *ibid.*
7. *The Baptist Handbook* (1894), p.154.
8. *The Baptist Handbook* (1922), pp.264–5.
9. *ibid.* (1865), p.121.
10. His obituary is to be found in *The Times*, 4 July 1884, p.11.
11. *The Baptist Handbook* (1990), pp.229–230.
12. *ibid.* (1902), pp.188–190.
13. *ibid.* (1900), pp.236–8.
14. Spurgeon's College Annual Report (1870), pp.4–10.
15. C.H. Spurgeon, *Autobiography* (1890) vol.2, p.142.

NOTES

16. *ibid.* p.145.
17. J. Duckett and A. Sternberg working for the British Society for the Propagation of the Gospel among the Jews.
18. No.1437, Application form, June 1890.
19. No.1437, 23 June 1890.
20. No.1437, 28 June 1890.
21. No.1437, 17 June 1890.
22. No.1437, 26 June 1890.
23. No.1437, 24 June 1890.
24. No.1437, 17 June 1890.
25. No.1437.
26. No.1437, 24 June 1890.
27. *The Sword and the Trowel* (1882), p.261.
28. *ibid.* (1881), p.309.
29. *ibid.* (1887), p.205.
30. No records exist giving ages of students but from a photograph of the batch for 1883 it is clear that the average age was late twenties. Writing in 1885 Spurgeon indicated that 'good men already in pastorates, earnest, useful, plodding but conscious of a great lack...have come to us and they have made the best of students because they have known by experience the value of knowledge.' He puts the number as 'several' and such men inevitably raised the average age of the students. *The Sword and the Trowel* (1885), p.206.
31. *The Sword and the Trowel* (1881), p.303.
32. There were four terms a year with two weeks vacation at Christmas, a month in midsummer and a week at the end of the other quarters. *The Baptist Handbook* (1868), p.24.
33. The following summary of numbers was made in 1883:

Number of brethren who have been educated in the College	652
• now in our ranks as Pastors, Missionaries and Evangelists	486
• without Pastorates but regularly engaged in the work of the Lord	9
• not now engaged in the work (secular callings)	19
• Medical Missionary Students	3
• Educated for other Denominations	2
• Dead (Pastors, 38; Students, 6)	44
• Permanently invalided	5
• Names removed from the List for various reasons, such as joining other Denominations, etc.	64

34. 'The foremost among our aims is the promotion of a vigorous spiritual life.... By frequent meetings for prayer and by other means we labour to maintain a high tone of spirituality. I have endeavoured in my lectures to stir up the holy fire; for well I know that if the heavenly flame burns low nothing else will avail.' *The Sword and the Trowel* (1881), p.304.
35. 'Everything is done to flourish the spirit of devotion. The tutors and students form a species of Protestant fraternity of the ancient type with all its good.' *The British Standard*, 8 February 1863.
36. *The Sword and the Trowel* (1882), p.309.
37. *Annual Report* (1886), p.20.
38. *The Sword and the Trowel* (1881), p.487.
39. J.A. Spurgeon, *The Sword and the Trowel* (1882), p.269.

40. *The Sword and the Trowel* (1883), p.31.
41. *ibid.* (1883), p.284.
42. *Annual Report* (1866), p.32.
43. *The Sword and the Trowel* (1886), p.309.
44. *ibid.* (1885), pp.205-210.
45. *Theological Lectures by Mr Gracey, Pastors' College, beginning August 20th, 1879.* Spurgeon's College Archives.
46. *ibid.* p.6.
47. These reasons are:
    1. Because the gospel is a remedial system
    2. The subject is nearer to us than others.
    3. Sin first engages the mind of the enquirer after salvation.
    4. This is the divine order in Genesis.
48. *ibid.* p.34.
49. *ibid.* p.36.
50. *ibid.* p.56.
51. *ibid.* p.141.
52. This is deposited in the Spurgeon's College Archives.
53. *The Sword and the Trowel* (1888), p.316.
54. All this material is taken from an unheaded unnumbered book giving records of the Discussion Class 1868-71. Spurgeon's College Archives.
55. For example nine 'Obstacles of Soul Winning' are listed:
    1. Indifference and Levity; 2. Unbelief; 3. Delay; 4. Carnal security; 5. Despair; 6. Love of Sin; 7. Self-righteousness; 8. Worldliness; 9. Habits and Company. E.R. Pullen, *Notes on C.H. Spurgeon's Lectures*, 1886-7, p.20.
56. This Assessment Book is kept in the College Archives and a typical page records these facts: Name—Address in London—Comments of Tutors: J.A. Spurgeon, D. Gracey, A. Fergusson, F.G. Marchant—Date and place of settlement.
57. Carlile, p.169.
58. *The Puritan Preacher in the Nineteenth Century. A Boston Monograph* (1893).
59. *The Sword and the Trowel* (1890), p.317. This visitation had been undertaken since at least 1867. In that year 'brethren worked in 47 districts, visited 2,121 houses, 3,777 families and distributed 4,027 sermons. In addition the public houses were visited with uniform kindness by the landlords.' *Annual Report*, 1867, pp.50-55.
60. *ibid.* p.323.
61. *Annual Report* (1889), p.313.
62. J. Stuart, *Sketch of the Life and Work of the Rev. W. Hobbs*, pp.8-10.
63. *Annual Report* (1877), pp.3-5.
64. *Annual Report* (1866), pp.36-7.
65. *ibid.* p.5.
66. *Annual Report* (1867), pp.36-7.
67. *ibid.* (1873), p.6.
68. *The Sword and the Trowel* (1888), p.316.
69. *ibid.* p.311.
70. *ibid.* p.317.
71. Six students were sent on to Edinburgh University and another to study medicine for missionary work. All received financial aid.
72. *Annual Report* (1871), p.4.

NOTES

73. Carlile, pp.174–5.
74. Printed letter dated 6 November 1886 addressed 'Beloved Friends', and signed Spurgeon. College Archives.
75. *Annual Report* (1866), pp.60–68.
76. *ibid.* (1868), p.39.
77. *The Sword and the Trowel* (1882), p.263.
78. *ibid.* (1881), p.133.
79. *Annual Report* (1866), p.43.
80. Detailed accounts appear in the works of Carlile and Fullerton. There is a polemical account by Iain Murray, called *The Forgotten Spurgeon* (Edinburgh, 1956). Sir James Marchant has written the story from accounts by Clifford and a former colleague, Dr Watkins, now lost. There is a brief section in A.C. Underwood, *A History of the English Baptists* (1947), pp.229–232; and in W.B. Glover, *Evangelical Nonconformists and Higher Criticism in the Nineteenth Century* (1954). The fullest accounts have been written by E.A. Payne. One is in Chapter 7 of *The Baptist Union: A Short History* (1959), based on an unpublished account deposited in the Angus Library, Oxford. A later article, paying special attention to the evidence of contemporary letters, appeared in the *Baptist Quarterly*, October 1979, pp.146–58. The most recent account is by P.S. Kruppa, *Charles Haddon Spurgeon: A Preacher's Progress* (New York, 1982), chapter 8. There is an outline of events in *The Freeman*, 20 April, 1888, pp.251–5.
81. M.K. Nicholls, 'The Downgrade Controversy: A Neglected Protagonist', *Baptist Quarterly*, 32, April 1988, pp.260–274, and M.T.E. Hopkins, 'Spurgeon's Opponents in the Downgrade Controversy', *Baptist Quarterly*, 32, April 1988, pp.274–294.
82. 'We, as a body of men, believe in "the doctrines of grace"—what are popularly styled Calvinistic views. We feel that we could not receive into this our union any who do not unfeignedly believe that salvation is all of the free grace of God from first to last, and is not according to human merit, but by the undeserved favour of God. We believe in the eternal purpose of the Father, the finished redemption of the Son, and the effectual work of the Holy Ghost.' (Minutes of College Conference).
83. Conference Minute Book, April 1888—January 1909, p.1.
84. *The Sword and the Trowel* (1888), pp.312–320.
85. Charles Williams, *The National Baptist*, Philadelphia, 31 May 1888.
86. *Christian World*, 23 February 1888.
87. *ibid.*
88. *Faith's Witness*, 16 December 1863, pp.7–10. Five left in 1859; five in 1860; four in 1861; 11 in 1862 and 13 in 1863.
89. *The Sword and the Trowel* (1881), p.306.
90. Letter to Subscribers 1868—from *Annual Report* (1869).
91. *The Sword and the Trowel* (1866), p.3.
92. W.T. Whitley, *The Baptists of London* (1928), p.79.
93. Carlile, p.171.
94. L.F. Higgs, *The Story of Trinity, Bexleyheath* (1968), p.16.
95. *Annual Report* (1879), p.24.
96. *ibid.* p.4.
97. *ibid.* p.8.
98. *The Sword and the Trowel* (1883), p.281.

99. C.H. Spurgeon, *Autobiography* (1890), vol.1, p.182.

Chapter 3: The Tabernacle

1. Annual Report of the Pastors' College 1891/2 incorporated in *The Sword and the Trowel* (1891/2), pp.335-6.
2. Annual Report of the Pastors' College 1893/4 incorporated in *The Sword and the Trowel* (1893), pp.305 & 308.
3. Annual Report of the Pastors' College 1894/5 incorporated in *The Sword and the Trowel* (1894/5), p.307.
4. Annual Report of the Pastors' College 1908/9 incorporated in *The Sword and the Trowel* (1908/9), p.300.
5. P.S. Kruppa, *Charles Haddon Spurgeon: A Preacher's Progress* (Columbia, 1982), p.116.
6. J.C. Carlile, *C.H. Spurgeon: An Interpretative Biography* (1933), p.109.
7. Kruppa, *op.cit.* p.176.
8. Carlile, *op.cit.* p.298.
9. Soham Church Book, p.86. Dr Willams' Library.
10. Copies of all the Baptist Handbooks are in Baptist House, Didcot.
11. For a comparative study of six London Colleges, two Church of England (King's and London College of Divinity), two Baptist (Stepney/Regent's Park and Spurgeon's), one Methodist (Richmond), and one Congregationalist (Homerton/New College), see M.K. Nicholls, London M. Phil dissertation 1990, 'Ministerial Training in London 1830-1890: A Comparative Study.'
12. Spurgeon's College examination paper, Midsummer 1916, Spurgeon's College Heritage Room.
13. For a full discussion, see: 'Oxford tutors and their professional critic', *Fortnightly Review*, 47 (January-June 1890) pp.294-6; J.E. Thorold Rogers, 'Oxford Professors and Oxford Tutors', *Fortnightly Review*, 56 (July-December 1889), p.934; 'University Organisation' by A. Don, *Fraser's Magazine*, 77 (February 1868), pp.135-159; 'Protest against Examinations', *The Nineteenth Century*, 24 (1888), pp.617-37; T. Fowler, 'On Examinations', *Fortnightly Review*, 19 (new set, 1876), pp.418-29; 'Oxford professors and Oxford tutors: reply of the examiners in the School of Modern History', *Contemporary Review*, 57 (January-June 1890), pp.183-6.
14. Annual Report of the Pastors' College 1893/94 incorporated in *The Sword and the Trowel* (1894), pp.303.
15. *ibid*.
16. Annual Report of the Pastors' College 1894/5 incorporated in *The Sword and the Trowel* (1895), pp.306.
17. Annual Report of the Pastors' College 1896/7 incorporated in *The Sword and the Trowel* (1897), pp.305-9.
18. Pastors' College Minute Book 1898-1930. Minutes of the meeting of the Trustees 25th June 1908, Spurgeon's College Archives. Annual Report of the Pastors' College 1908/9 incorporated in *The Sword and the Trowel* (1909), p.300.
19. *ibid*. Minutes of meeting of College Trustees 10 February 1910. Spurgeon's College Archives. See also Annual Report of the Pastors' College 1900/10 incorporated in *The Sword and the Trowel* (1910), pp.302.

NOTES

20. Pastors' College Minute Books 1893–1898, 1898–1930. Spurgeon's College Archives.
21. Annual Report of the Pastors' College 1809/10 incorporated in *The Sword and the Trowel* (1910), pp.302–303.
22. Annual Report of the Pastors' College 1894/5 incorporated in *The Sword and the Trowel* (1895), p.306.
23. Annual Report of the Pastors' College 1906/7 incorporated in *The Sword and the Trowel* (1907), p.300.
24. Pastors' College Minute Book 1898–1930. Minutes of meeting of the College Trustees 13 October 1911. Spurgeon's College Archives.
25. *ibid*. Minutes of the joint meetings of the College Trustees and the College Conference Committee on 9 and 16 March 1917. See also Minutes of the meeting of the College Trustees on 23 November 1916, and the notes of a joint committee of the College Trustees and the Conference Committee on 15 December 1916. Spurgeon's College Archives.
26. *ibid*. Minutes of a special meeting of the College Trustees on 4 March 1909. Spurgeon's College Archives.
27. *ibid*. Minutes of meeting of College Committee on 11 June 1919.
28. *ibid*. Minutes of meeting of College Council on 25 January 1924. Spurgeon's College Archives.
29. *ibid*. Minutes of meeting of College Committee on 25 March 1920. Spurgeon's College Archives.
30. Spurgeon's College Calendar, 1924.
31. Pastors' College Minute Book 1898–1930. Minutes of meeting of College Council on 11 May 1922. Spurgeon's College.
32. Estate Agent's brochure describing Freehold Residential Estate known as Falkland Park. Spurgeon's College Archives.
33. Pastors' College Minute Book 1898–1930. Financial Appeal leaflet inserted in Minutes of College Council meeting on 14 December 1922. Spurgeon's College Archives.
34. *The Sword and the Trowel*, vol.57, No. 715 October 1923, p.750.
35. Spurgeon's College Annual Reports 1910–1939. Annual Paper 1923/4. Spurgeon's College Archives.

Chapter 4: The Brethren

1. Presidential Address of Spurgeon's College Conference in the Centenary Year of his birth in loyalty to the Spurgeon tradition, pp.17–19.
2. Spurgeon's College Record, April, 1953—December 1960. June 1959, No.28, p.5. Spurgeon's College Archives.
3. Spurgeon's College Record, April, 1948—December 1952. December 1959, No.9, pp.27–29. Spurgeon's College Archives.
4. *ibid*. August 1948, No.2, pp.5–7. Spurgeon's College Archives.
5. Spurgeon's College Magazine. February 1927, No.2, p.10. Spurgeon's College Archives.
6. Spurgeon's College Magazine No.3, undated but probably September 1927. Spurgeon's College Archives.
7. Spurgeon's College Record, April, 1948—December 1952. August 1951, No.11, pp.2–3. Spurgeon's College Archives.

8. Spurgeon's College Record, April, 1953—December 1960. December 1953, No.17, p.15. Spurgeon's College Archives.
9. *ibid*. December 1957, No. 25, pp.17–19. Spurgeon's College Archives.
10. Spurgeon's College Record, April 1953—December 1960. September 1956, No.22, p.7. Spurgeon's College Archives.
11. Spurgeon's College Record, April 1948—December 1960. June 1958, No.26, pp.14–16. Spurgeon's College Archives.
12. Spurgeon's College Record, April 1948—December 1952. August 1951, No.11, pp.4–5. Spurgeon's College Archives.
13. Spurgeon's College Record. December 1978, No.67, p.6. Spurgeon's College Archives.
14. Spurgeon's College Minute Book 1946—1961. Minutes of Council meeting 28 June 1946. Spurgeon's College Archives.
15. *ibid*. Minutes of Council Meeting 16/17 June 1949. Spurgeon's College Archives.
16. Spurgeon's College Record, April 1953—December 1960. December 1954, No.19, pp.17–18. Spurgeon's College Archives.
17. Spurgeon's College Annual Reports 1910—1939. Report for 1927/8, p.2. Spurgeon's College Archives.
18. Spurgeon's College Record, April 1953—December 1960. June 1956, No.22, p.36. Spurgeon's College Archives.
19. *ibid*. June 1958, No.26, pp.2–3. Spurgeon's College Archives.
20. Curriculum No.1. Spurgeon's College Archives.
21. Spurgeon's College Annual Reports 1910—1939. Spurgeon's College Archives.
22. Spurgeon's College Record, April 1948—December 1952. April 1949, No.4, pp.23–26. Spurgeon's College Archives.
23. *ibid*. December 1948, No.3, pp.6–8. Spurgeon's College Archives.

Chapter 5: The Ministry

1. Minutes of Special Council Meeting, held on Wednesday, 4th September, 1957.
2. For a fuller appreciation of G.R. Beasley-Murray, see J.J. Brown's contribution in *Mission to the World* ed. Paul Beasley-Murray ('Baptist Historical Society', 1991).

Bibliography

Alleine, *Alarm to Sinners*.
Anon., *Charles Haddon Spurgeon: A Biographical Sketch And Appreciation by One Who Knew Him Well*, (1903).
Anon., *The Puritan Preacher in the Nineteenth Century. A Boston Monograph*, (1893).
Anon., 'Bampfield's Plan for an Educated Ministry', *Transactions of the Baptist Historical Society*, 3, 1912–13, p.17.
Anon., 'Sutcliff's Academy at Olney, *Baptist Quarterly*, 6, 1932–33, p.124.
Anon., 'The General Baptist Academy of the Old Connexion', *Baptist Quarterly*, 3, 1926–27, pp.331–2.
Anon., 'Oxford tutors and their professional critic', *Fortnightly Review*, 47, (January–June 1890), pp.294–6.
Anon., 'Protest against Examinations', *The Nineteenth Century*, 24, (1888), pp.617–37.
Arnold, Matthew, *St Paul & Protestantism, With an Essay on Puritanism & The Church of England*.
Ashley-Smith, J.W., *Birth of Education*.
Baxter, *Call to the Unconverted*.
Brook, W., 'John Ward, LLD, FRS, FSA', *Transactions of the Baptist Historical Society*, 4, 1914–15, p.26.
Brown, Kenneth, *A Social History of the Nonconformist Ministry in England and Wales*. Oxford, 1988.
Campbell, J.M., *The Nature of the Atonement*, Sixth Edition.
Carlile, J.C., *C.H. Spurgeon: An Interpretative Biography*, (1933).
Clifford, John, *The English Baptists*, (1881).
Cooper, R.E., *From Stepney to St Giles*.
Davies, Horton, *Worship and Theology in England*, 4 vols., (1962).
Doddridge, Philip, *The Rise and Progress of Religion in the Soul*.
Don, A., 'University Organisation, 77, (February 1868), pp.135–159.
Farrar, F.W., *Eternal Hope*.
Fowler, T., 'On Examinations', *Fortnightly Review*, 19, (new set, 1876), pp.418–29.
Fullerton, W.Y., *C.H. Spurgeon: A Biography* (1920).
Glover, W.B., *Evangelical Nonconformists and Higher Criticism in the Nineteenth-Century*, (1954).
Gould, G.P., *The Baptist College at Regent's Park: A Century Record*, (1910).
Gummer, S., 'Trosnant Academy'. *Baptist Quarterly*, 9, 1938–39.
Harte, F.W., *Historical Tablets of the Pastors' College*.
Higgs, L.F., *The Story of Trinity, Bexleyheath*, (1968).
Himbury, B.M., *Baptist Quarterly*, 21, No.8, 1966, p.340.
Hopkins, M.T.E., 'Spurgeon's Opponents in the Downgrade Controversy', *Baptist Quarterly*, 32, April 1988, pp.274–294.
Ivimey,, *History of the English Baptists*, vol.1, (1811).

James, J.A., *Anxious Enquirer.*
Johnson, W.C., *Encounter in London* (1965).
Kent, John, *Holding the Fort* (1978).
Kruppa, P.S., *Charles Haddon Spurgeon: A Preacher's Progress* New York, (1982).
Maurice, F.D., *Theological Essays* Fifth Edition.
Moon, N., *Education for Ministry* (1979).
Murray, Iain, *The Forgotten Spurgeon* (Edinburgh, 1956).
Nicholls, M.K., 'The Downgrade Controversy: A Neglected Protagonist', *Baptist Quarterly*, 32, April 1988, pp.260-274.
Payne, E.A., *The Baptist Union: A Short History* (1959).
Payne, E.A., *The Free Church Tradition in the Life of England.*
Pike, G.H., *The Life and Work of Charles Haddon Spurgeon*, 4 vols., (1892).
Price, E.J., 'Dissenting Academies, 1661-1820', *Baptist Quarterly*, 6, 1932-33, p.135.
Pullen, E.R., *Notes on C.H. Spurgeon's Lectures, 1886-7.*
Regent's Park College, *Annual Report*, (1853, 1885).
Rogers, J.E.T., 'Oxford Professors and Oxford Tutors', *Fortnightly Review*, 56, (July—December 1889), p.934.
Rogers, J.E.T., 'Oxford Professors and Oxford Tutors: reply of the examiners in the School of Modern History', *Contemporary Review*, 57, (January-June 1890), pp.183-6.
Spurgeon, C.H., *Autobiography*, 4 vols., (1890).
Spurgeon, C.H., *Lectures to My Students*, 3 vols., (1877, 1893, 1894).
Spurgeon, C.H., *The New Park Street Pulpit*, 1855-1860, (1863-4).
Spurgeon, C.H., *The Metropolitan Tabernacle Pulpit, (1863-1917, containing sermons preached and revised by Spurgeon at the Metropolitan Tabernacle from 1861 until his death in 1892*, 54 vols.
Spurgeon's College, *Annual Report*, (1866, 1867, 1868, 1869, 1870, 1871, 1877, 1879, 1881, 1886, 1889, 1892).
Stuart, J., *Sketch of the Life and Work of the Rev. W. Hobbs.*
The Baptist Handbook, (1862, 1868, 1894, 1900, 1902, 1922).
Thielicke, T., *Encounter with Spurgeon.*
Tongue, E.J., 'Dr John Ward's Trust', *Baptist Quarterly*, 4, 1949-50, p.221.
Underwood, A.C., *A History of the English Baptists* (1947).
Valentine, T.F., *Concern for the Ministry: The Story of the Particular Baptist Fund, 1717-1967.*
Whitley, W.T., *The Baptists of London* (1928).
Williams, Charles, *The National Baptist* Philadelphia, (1888).
Williams, William, *Personal Reminiscences of C.H. Spurgeon* (1895).
Wilson, W., *History and Antiquities of Dissenting Churches and Meeting Houses in London, Westminster and Southwark*, vol.2, (1810).